T0208590

Building the Commune

The Jacobin series features short interrogations of politics, economics, and culture from a socialist perspective, as an avenue to radical political practice. The books offer critical analysis and engagement with the history and ideas of the Left in an accessible format.

The series is a collaboration between Verso Books and *Jacobin* magazine, which is published quarterly in print and online at jacobinmag.com.

Other titles in this series available from Verso Books:

The New Prophets of Capital by Nicole Aschoff
Playing the Whore by Melissa Gira Grant
Utopia or Bust by Benjamin Kunkel
Strike for America by Micah Uetricht
Class War by Megan Erickson
Four Futures by Peter Frase

Building the Commune

Radical Democracy in Venezuela

GEORGE CICCARIELLO-MAHER

VERSO

London • New York

This edition first published by Verso 2016
© George Ciccariello-Maher 2016

3 5 7 9 10 8 6 4 2

Verso
UK: 6 Meard Street, London W1F 0EG
US: 388 Atlantic Ave, Brooklyn, NY 11217
versobooks.com

Verso is the imprint of New Left Books

ISBN-13; 978-1-78478-223-8
ISBN-13: 978-1-78478-224-5 (US EBK)
ISBN-13: 978-1-78478-225-2 (UK EBK)

British Library Cataloguing in Publication Data
A catalogue record for this book is available from the British Library

Library of Congress Cataloging-in-Publication Data
A catalog record for this book is available from the Library of Congress

Typeset in Fournier by Hewer Text UK Ltd, Edinburgh, Scotland
Printed in the United States

CONTENTS

INTRODUCTION

Nothing says "enough" like a bus on fire. On February 27, 1989, Venezuelans woke up to an economic reform package that saw gas prices double overnight, and with them bus fares. Workers and students on their Monday morning commute into the capital, Caracas, decided they had had enough. Instead of simply paying the new fare, they began to burn buses, occupy bus terminals, and block streets. While their anger was initially focused on the bus drivers, it wasn't long before they set their sights on the government. Burning buses soon gave way to marches and protests, broken glass, looted stores, and nearly a week of rioting across the entire country.

Grainy news footage from the rebellion shows the population looting unashamedly, some covering their faces but most not even bothering. After all, they were taking back things they deserved, but of which they had been deprived. Basic goods that had become too expensive or hard to find were soon discovered hoarded in warehouses and storerooms. These were now redistributed directly by the people themselves, who carried everything from imported whiskey to entire sides of beef on their shoulders up into the *barrios* (shantytowns) surrounding the city. In some instances, local police—who knew full well they couldn't stop the looting if they tried—even helped to make the process more orderly.

This was the Caracazo—the "explosion in Caracas," although the rebellion quickly went national, lasting almost a full week in some places. The Caracazo marked the first of a series of Latin American rebellions against the spread of neoliberal economic reforms that would see presidents deposed and political parties collapse across the continent. In theory, neoliberalism claims to minimize the role of the state in favor of the free market, but in practice the state has played a major role in enforcing neoliberal reform at gunpoint, in Latin America and elsewhere. When Augusto Pinochet overthrew Salvador Allende, the elected socialist president of Chile, in a 1973 coup backed by the CIA, he made the country a testing ground for radical experiments in market-based economics. And in the 1980s, a US interest-rate increase set off a debt crisis across Latin America as a whole that provided a pretext for the International Monetary Fund (IMF) and the World Bank to step in and impose neoliberal reforms more broadly.[1]

Poor countries saddled with massive debts had no choice but to beg the IMF and World Bank for bailouts. The strings attached to these loans took the form of what has been called

---

1   David Harvey, *A Brief History of Neoliberalism* (Oxford: Oxford University Press, 2007), 29.

"structural adjustment," but this polite term conceals a brutal reality. In practice, neoliberal reforms meant cutting wages, laying off teachers and other public-sector workers, cutting social-welfare spending, and privatizing public goods by selling off natural resources and services like water and gas—not to the highest bidder, but often to the highest briber. Under duress from international lenders, governments handed over their sovereignty by restructuring entire economies according to the dictates of the global market, giving foreign corporations free rein while they paid almost no taxes, and eliminating any and all price controls put in place to protect the poorest Latin Americans.

In Venezuela, gas prices and bus fares were simply the last straw. Following a decade of oil-fueled growth, the Venezuelan economy had been in crisis since at least 1983, when the price of oil tanked and the currency devalued sharply, instantly making people's wages and the money in their pockets worth much less. One newspaper greeted the decision, whose date is still known as Black Friday, with a headline announcing: "The Party Is Over."[2] A series of neoliberal reform packages followed, with a single common denominator: eliminating all safeguards that existed to protect the Venezuelan population from the ravages of the global economy. This meant lifting price controls on the basic goods the population needed, freeing interest rates,

---

2 Here and in what follows, I rely on Margarita López Maya, *Del viernes negro al referendo revocatorio* (Caracas: Alfadil, 2005).

reducing all sorts of subsidies—gas prices included—and increasing the cost of public utilities.

The result in Venezuela and elsewhere was not the growth that neoliberal economists and ideologues had promised, but instead the exact opposite: what is referred to in Latin America as the "lost decade," in which the only things that really grew were unemployment and poverty. By the end of the 1980s, nearly half of all Latin Americans were living in poverty, with nearly 70 million falling into poverty in that decade alone. By 1989, the Venezuelan economy was shrinking, inflation was running at 85 percent, and the poor were bearing the brunt: more than 44 percent of families were living in poverty, and almost half of those in extreme poverty.

Against this backdrop, presidential candidate Carlos Andrés Pérez played the role of charismatic savior. Having presided over an oil boom during his first term as president in the early 1970s, Pérez was a reminder of the good old days, and he made big promises to match. His 1988 electoral campaign echoed popular frustrations with the emerging international financial system that was saddling poor countries with debts they couldn't pay. Pérez denounced the IMF as a "bomb that only kills people," accused the World Bank of "genocide," and encouraged collective resistance among indebted nations worldwide. Once elected, however, Pérez did a sharp about-face: in exchange for billions of dollars in IMF loans, he signed on to a structural adjustment plan even more radical than those of his predecessors.

When rebellion is in the air, however, broken promises can be fatal, and the widespread perception that Pérez had betrayed his own campaign promises, in what many characterized as a "bait and switch," had everything to do with the fury Venezuelans would unleash in the streets during the Caracazo. Pérez repaid that fury in kind. Unable to quell the rioting by other means, he declared a state of emergency and sent the army and police into the barrios surrounding the capital to subdue the rebellious poor. Young army recruits sprayed entire apartment blocks with automatic gunfire, killing many who lived and looked just like themselves, leaving bullet holes that are still visible today. In a single incident, the army opened fire on a crowd gathered on the Mesuca stairway in the poor slum of Petare in eastern Caracas, killing more than twenty. When all was said and done, hundreds if not thousands had been slaughtered—the numbers have never been agreed upon because bodies were simply dumped into the mass graves that are still being unearthed today.

Given the brutal failure of neoliberal reforms across the region as a whole, the Caracazo would soon be followed by a string of rebellions elsewhere on the continent and beyond. Only a year after the Caracazo, indigenous movements in Ecuador responded to neoliberal reform with the Inti Raymi uprising (1990), unleashing a chain reaction that would eventually see three sitting presidents unseated from power by street mobilizations. The Zapatista rebellion in southern Mexico (1994) exploded into history on the same day that the North American Free Trade Agreement (NAFTA) took effect, provoked by the Mexican government's abolition of communal land rights to please the United States, and has

since helped to inspire struggles worldwide while undermin-
ing the legitimacy of a corrupt political system. Struggles in
Bolivia against attempts to privatize first water (2000), and
then gas (2003), led to the removal of two presidents.

These grassroots rebellions did more than simply destroy,
however. Through resistance to neoliberalism, new movements emerged, new alternatives were forged, and new
leaders were thrown into power: Hugo Chávez in Venezuela,
Evo Morales in Bolivia, and Rafael Correa in Ecuador all
contributed to the broader leftward swing in the region, later
dubbed the "Pink Tide." Even more importantly, new forms
of democracy also emerged that were local, participatory,
direct, and communal—in short, unrecognizable from the
perspective of the old, corrupt form of democracy in crisis
throughout the region.

For example, when the state failed to provide drinking
water to communities in Cochabamba, Bolivia, residents did
not look for solutions through elections but took matters into
their own hands. They came together to dig wells and manage
the water supply themselves in a participatory and democratic way that built on both indigenous and leftist traditions.
When water rights were later sold off to the transnational
corporation Bechtel, these same neighborhood organizations
barricaded the entire city to collectively resist the move,
sparking a chain of events that has transformed the country
as a whole.

These new experiments in democracy have since gone
global, with the Spanish *indignados*, Tahrir Square protesters,
and Occupy Wall Street all fighting against neoliberalism

through practices of direct discussion, debate, and management of our own lives. Some would call this new form of self-government "direct democracy" or "radical democracy"; others might insist that it is the only democracy truly worthy of the name. What this developing form of self-government could look like is not yet clear, in part because it seeks to respond to an unavoidable challenge: how to harness the spontaneous energy of rebellion into new forms of political organizing, and how to ensure that these forms don't betray their rebellious origins.

In Venezuela, the rejection of neoliberalism in the streets during the Caracazo led not only to Chávez's election, but also to a long and continuing experiment in radical democracy that continues to this day in new institutions of local self-government, known as communes. At the time of the Caracazo, Chávez and others had been conspiring both within the army and alongside clandestine revolutionary groups, but the spontaneous rebellion by the people in the streets caught them off guard and forced them into action. On February 4, 1992, the Revolutionary Bolivarian Movement attempted to depose Pérez in a coup d'état that failed to seize power but made Chávez a national hero overnight.

It was only through the combined impact of the Caracazo and the failed coup that Chávez would later be elected president in December 1998, amid the collapse of the corrupt two-party system. The first task of his new government was to fulfill the most important promise of the electoral campaign: rewriting the Venezuelan Constitution. Within six months of Chávez's inauguration in early 1999, a constituent assembly was elected, and before the year was out the Bolivarian Constitution had been approved in a national referendum. The new Constitution, written with the participation of social movements and grassroots Bolivarian Circles, promised to expand both social welfare and participatory democracy.

Social welfare came first, with the Bolivarian government attempting to tackle the poverty and social exclusion left by more than a decade of neoliberal reform. But even after being elected, the Chávez government lacked control over the purse strings of the national oil company, Petróleos de Venezuela, S.A. (PDVSA). As a result, the revolution would not truly get under way until the combative whirlwind that began with the brief coup against Chávez in April 2002. US-backed and -funded opposition forces briefly kidnapped the president and abolished the new Constitution before being forced out of power by mass mobilizations in the streets and the barracks alike. Defeated politically but not economically, opposition forces then shut down the entire Venezuelan oil industry in late 2002. They were again defeated, this time by oil workers who seized the installations after more than two catastrophic months.

With oil production now firmly in the hands of the state, the Bolivarian government sought to make good on its promises of social welfare, in particular through the establishment of a series of Bolivarian missions. Misión Barrio Adentro, for example, provided free health care in the poorest neighborhoods through Cuban-staffed medical clinics; a series of missions provided free education, from basic literacy training up to the university level; Misión Mercal provided subsidized food; Misión Vuelvan Caras (About-Face) sought to eradicate poverty by integrating the poorest of the poor— and these were followed by dozens more.

The effects of these policies on reversing the ravages of the neoliberal era have been undeniable: household poverty has been cut in half and extreme poverty cut by 63 percent. This doesn't even account for the impact—more difficult to measure—of expanded access to subsidized food and free health care and education. Venezuela went from being one of Latin America's most unequal countries to one of the most equal.[3] As the Bolivarian process radicalized, however, it began to move beyond social welfare and toward making good on the Constitution's promise of a more direct and participatory democracy. But the foundations of this radical democracy had been laid long before Chávez, by the residents of Venezuela's barrios themselves.

Today, well over 90 percent of Venezuelans live in the cities. If "perversion" literally means "turning away," the Venezuelan economy has been perverted since oil was discovered in the early twentieth century. Since then, the entire country has been reshaped, with political life turning away from the needs of society to face the global market, creating a vast geographic distortion in the process. Peasants abandoned an otherwise lush countryside for the cities, the majority coming to inhabit the

---

3 Mark Weisbrot, *Failed: What the "Experts" Got Wrong about the Global Economy* (Oxford: Oxford University Press, 2015), 218–20.

swelling barrios ringing urban areas. As Venezuelans rushed to the cities, agricultural production—indeed, all domestic production—plummeted. The contours of this perversion have everything to do with understanding the importance of the communes of today, as well as the challenges they face.

In Caracas, this process of urbanization was magnified by the oil economy: as the transit point for all wealth extracted from the subsoil, the capital city lured millions from the countryside with the symbolic glimmer of often-false promises of access to their share of the oil wealth. It was these new barrio residents—those who built informal housing in the hills while eking out a living through informal labor on the valley floor— who spearheaded the Caracazo rebellion of 1989. The collective identity and struggles emerging from the chaotic terrain of the barrios would lay the foundation for the new experiments in direct democracy.

For the most part, these were not factory workers squaring off against a boss in the workplace, but informal workers performing services or circulating the imported goods that flooded this oil economy. They confronted not a physical boss but the market itself, and their political demands centered not so much on where they *worked* but where they *lived*. As a result, in the words of Dario Azzellini, many "Venezuelans identify much more strongly with their community than with their workplace."[4] These are still very much workers in the

---

4   Dario Azzellini, "Workers' Control Under Venezuela's Bolivarian Revolution," in *Ours to Master and to Own: Workers' Control from the Commune to the Present*, edited by Immanuel Ness and Dario Azzellini (Chicago: Haymarket, 2011), 387.

broadest sense of the word, however, and in fact some of Venezuela's poorest, working without a contract and benefits, or hustling for a living in the unforgiving city.

Over time, their demands for running water, education, health care, stable streets and safe housing on unstable terrain, and cultural and sporting activities for youth all translated into new instruments of community control. And since Venezuelans were struggling against a corrupt, two-party system that was democratic only in name, it was natural that they would seek out more radically democratic ways to organize themselves. Neighbors formed associations and then spontaneous assemblies and popular self-defense militias in the 1980s and 1990s, especially after the Caracazo. They began to govern and defend their own communities—their own territories—by themselves.

It was these participatory, grassroots assemblies that served as the prototypes for what would come to be known as communal councils—officially recognized institutions for directly democratic self-government on the local level. And it was these councils—with the grassroots energy and territorial identity they embodied—that would later come together under the aegis of the broader units known as the communes.

In the chapters that follow, I track the emergence of the Venezuelan communes not only from above but from below. Just as Chávez the individual did not create the Bolivarian Revolution—it was instead the long revolutionary process that "created Chávez"—so too with the communes.[5] Before the Venezuelan state took on the task of building the communes from above, revolutionaries were building them from below. As a result, the relationship between the communes—the seeds of a future nonstate—and the existing state has been far from smooth.

I then turn to the ongoing struggle for urban space, to show how the urban movements that have always been the political spearhead of Chavismo are today fighting for a right to the city, storming earthly heavens by tearing down the walls separating the rich from the poor. If revolutionary Chavismo emerges from the space of the barrios, those who oppose it hail from the increasingly fortified zones housing the wealthy. In the third chapter, I analyze the opposition street protests of 2014, documenting the emergence of new right-wing movements that have skillfully appropriated tactics often associated with the left.

Next, I explain the dangerous clashes emerging within Chavismo today—offering no easy answers, simply an insistence on the creative powers of the revolutionary grassroots—before turning directly to the network of communes currently spreading across the Venezuelan political landscape. I do so with uncertainty but also with faith, both of which are essential for grasping a process that is still very much *in* process. The challenges confronting the communes are many, not least of which are the deepening

---

5   George Ciccariello-Maher, *We Created Chávez: A People's History of the Venezuelan Revolution* (Durham, NC: Duke University Press, 2013).

economic crisis and the political gains made by the opposition. But as a project for seizing and governing space to produce, the communes might just provide the best escape from the crisis. Marx once described the commune as the "form at last discovered" for the emancipation of workers, and that form is today being filled with the content of hundreds of thousands of revolutionaries who are making it their own in the construction of Venezuela's distinctively territorialized socialism.[6]

---

6 Karl Marx, *The Civil War in France*, in *The Marx-Engels Reader*, edited by Robert Tucker (New York: Norton, 1978), 635.

1

A HISTORY OF THE COMMUNE

By the time of his last major speech on October 20, 2012—soon after winning his final reelection—Hugo Chávez knew he was dying, but he looked as energetic as ever. His government ministers, on the other hand, looked sweaty and uncomfortable, with nowhere to hide as he chewed them out before the eyes of the nation, interrogating them on live television and demanding rectification for their mistakes. For more than three hours Chávez spoke, interspersed with commentary from ministers and on-the-ground reports from various sites on different aspects of the socialist project. He railed against government corruption, ineffectiveness, and inefficiency: "Will I continue to cry out in the desert?" he pleaded with increasing exasperation.

This speech would come to be known as the "Golpe de Timón," which literally means "Strike at the Helm" but suggests a radical change in course.[1] The change in question

---

1   An English translation of most of this speech is available from *Monthly Review*: monthlyreview.org/commentary/strike-at-the-helm/.

was the transition to socialism itself, long promised but only partially delivered. It's too easy, Chávez insisted, to simply call things "socialist" without changing their fundamental structure. Since he had come to power, social welfare had improved dramatically, but the 1999 Constitution promised *more*: more participation, more democracy, more equality, and a new Venezuela. By 2006, this ambitious project had a name—"twenty-first-century socialism"—and it entailed far more than simply improving social welfare or reducing poverty: the goal was to transform political power itself to create something "truly new." For Chávez, socialism was not opposed to democracy but instead *synonymous* with it: "Socialism *is* democracy and democracy *is* socialism."

The building blocks for this new socialist democracy were the communal councils, established in a 2006 law. These councils—directly democratic and participatory institutions for local governance—quickly numbered in the thousands as neighbors began to come together weekly to debate and discuss how to govern themselves. Whether in a dingy room adorned with little more than a poster or mural of Chávez, or outside around a collective stew pot, the debates ranged from banal to engaging, from the local to the national and everything in between. Whether it is building new roads and basketball courts, or strategizing how to deal with increasing drug violence, these councils have become crucial spaces for political participation in Venezuela today. But as late as 2012, it was not entirely clear what this new form of socialism would look like or how to build it. Would the role of the councils be limited to local development? Would they serve as a check on the power of the central government? Or were they instead destined to be a part of something far more ambitious?

For Chávez, the answer was increasingly clear: capitalism was a "monster" that would swallow up any and all small, local alternatives, and a radical leap toward socialism was needed if the Bolivarian process was not to come to an abrupt halt. This meant that the communal councils, not to mention other cooperative or socialist enterprises, were doomed on their own. For the councils to provide a true counterweight to the corruption and bureaucracy of the oil state, they would need to be unified and consolidated into something much bigger. This something was the communes themselves, legally established in a 2010 law designed to bring the communal councils and other participatory units together in increasingly larger self-governed areas. Two years later, however, not a single commune had been established, leading the president to emphasize one question above all: "Where is the commune?"

The question was for his government ministers, and they had no answer. "We keep distributing homes, but the communes are nowhere to be seen." This was not only a question of the absence of legally registered communes, but something far deeper: What was still lacking, according to Chávez, was "the *spirit* of the commune which is much more important, communal *culture*." The error of government ministers was not that they had failed to create communes from above, but that they had forgotten that those communes needed to be born from below: "The commune—popular power—does not come from Miraflores Palace, nor is it from such and such ministry that we will be able to solve our problems."

If Chávez had addressed his question—"Where is the commune?"—to those grassroots organizers who have always been the backbone of Chavismo, the answer might have been very different. Some would have no doubt pointed to the very ground on which they stood, as though to say: The commune is *here*, Comandante.

While the councils and communes were enshrined by law in 2006 and 2010, it is a mistake to think that the Venezuelan state created the communes or the communal councils that they comprise. Just as Chávez did not create the Bolivarian Revolution, the revolutionary movements that "created Chávez" did not simply stop there and stand back to admire their creation. Instead, they continued their formative work in and on the world by building radically democratic and participatory self-government from the bottom up.

In the 1980s, long before the communal councils existed on paper and before Chávez had become a household name, barrio residents—struggling for local autonomy against corrupt two-party rule—began forming a network of barrio assemblies to debate both local affairs and how to bring about revolutionary change on the national level. Before the communes existed on paper, many of these same organizers had begun to expand and consolidate communal control over broader swathes of territory. In fact, one of the most important organizations building communal power in the present—the National Network of *Comuneros* and *Comuneras*—was founded by former state employees who broke away in favor of a more independent organization. As Marx and others have, "revolutions are not made with laws" but by the people seizing and exercising power directly.[2]

These communes have existed since the very moment when those who gathered in their neighborhood councils said *this is not enough*. It is not enough to govern this little corner of Venezuela or that little fragment of the barrio. It is not enough to make decisions about streets and water pipes while there is a broader battle to be fought. It is not enough to have direct democracy in a four-block radius while everything the neighborhood consumes is trucked in from a distance, much of it imported from abroad. It is not enough to be a tiny island of socialism in a vast capitalist sea. Local neighborhood councils would have to connect with one another; they would have to send delegates to discuss and debate questions on a larger scale: how to govern entire parishes, how to collaborate on security and infrastructure, and how to cooperate in the production and distribution of what communities actually need.

If the state did not create the communes, what the state has done is legally recognize the existence of first the councils and later the communes, formalizing their structure—for better and for worse—and even encouraging their expansion. Some

---

2   Karl Marx, *Capital: A Critique of Political Economy, Volume I*, translated by B. Fowkes (New York: Penguin, 1976), 915.

45,000 communal councils exist today, many of which have been incorporated into the now more than 1,500 communes. Within the state apparatus, these communes found no greater ally than Chávez himself, who, fully aware of his own pressing mortality, understood his "Golpe de Timón" as a sort of political will and testament. He knew that once he was gone, Chavistas of different loyalties and stripes would inevitably begin to fight over who best represented his legacy, and—if history is any guide—some would even use his name to betray that legacy. By dedicating his last major speech to the expansion of what he called the "communal state," Chávez was making perfectly clear that his legacy was the commune, giving radical organizers the leverage they needed to insist that to be a Chavista is to be a *comunero*, and that those who undermine popular power are no less than traitors.[3]

Today, no two communes look exactly alike. Sometimes a commune is sixty women gathered in a room to debate local road construction, berating political leaders in the harshest of terms. Other times it's a textile collective gathering with local residents to decide what the community needs and how best to produce it. Sometimes it's a handful of young men on motorcycles hammering out a gang truce, or others broadcasting on a collective radio or TV station. Often it's hundreds of rural families growing plantains, cacao, coffee,

---

3   In what follows, I do not translate *comunero* as either "communard"—whose reference to the Paris Commune is too direct—or as the more generic "commoner." Instead, to preserve its varied sources and inspirations, I leave the term in the original Spanish.

or corn while attempting to rebuild their ancestral dignity on the land through a new, collective form. There are some constants, however. The coffee is always too sweet, and the process is always difficult, endlessly messy and unpredictable in its inescapable creativity.

What is a commune? Concretely speaking, Venezuela's communes bring together communal councils—local units of direct democratic self-government—with productive units known as social property enterprises (EPS). Forming a commune is relatively straightforward: participants in a number of adjacent communal councils come together, discuss, and call a referendum among the entire local population. Once the commune is approved and constituted, each communal council and production unit sends an elected delegate to the communal parliament—the commune's highest decision-making body. Like the councils themselves, the parliament is based on principles of direct democracy. Anyone who is elected—just like all elected officials under the 1999 Constitution—is subject to community oversight and can be recalled from power. Communes even manage local security through participatory "collective defense," and an alternative system of communal justice seeks to resolve conflicts through "arbitration, conciliation, and mediation."[4]

Economically, communes are explicitly "socialist spaces," which means that they aim to produce the things that people

---

4   These and later citations are drawn from the Law of Communes and the Law for the Communal Economic System, both 2010. These and other laws related to communal power can be found at http://www.mpcomunas. gob.ve/leyes/.

need locally through socialist enterprises. These enterprises are explicitly noncapitalist and defined by who owns the means of production. They can be either state-owned or, more commonly, directly owned and managed by the communes themselves. Direct ownership means that the communal parliament itself—composed of delegates from each council—debates and decides what is produced, how much the workers are paid, how to distribute the product, and how best to reinvest any surplus into the commune itself.

The goal of the communes—with EPSs as their productive heart—is to build self-managed and sustainable communities that are oriented toward their own collective internal needs. But this local emphasis does not come at the expense of consolidating a broader communal power. Instead, the Commune Law points toward the integration of the communes into a broader regional and national confederation. The goal is ultimately to "build the communal state by promoting, driving, and developing . . . the exercise of self-government by the organized communities" and to construct "a system of production, distribution, exchange, and consumption rooted in social property."

As the communes expand across the national territory, the law also encourages them to claim greater authority over their local neighborhoods: building on Article 184 of the Constitution, the law allows the communes to demand the "transfer" of authority over privately held property to the communes themselves. As we will see, this ability to demand that private property be expropriated and handed over has become a key lever for the expansion of the communes and the overarching goal of "the transition toward a socialist and democratic society of equity and social justice."

The sources and inspirations for the Venezuelan commune are many, as any *comunero* or *comunera* will tell you. They include not only the Paris Commune of 1871 but also many more local movements before and since. Indigenous communities had long managed life collectively, and when Venezuelan slaves escaped to the hills to form maroon communities, these too often anticipated communal forms: participatory, direct, and self-governed. The long history of Venezuela's communes thus began long before Chávez and even before the great Latin American liberator Simón Bolívar helped to free the continent from Spanish domination at the outset of the nineteenth century. These experiments were not all the same, nor were they communes, strictly speaking, and some were more democratic than others. But each moment pointed toward the fundamental demand to control one's own everyday life, a search for the kind of collective power that Marx sought when he described the commune as the "self-government of the producers."[5]

As radical social movements and grassroots organizers in the barrios were experimenting with direct self-government through popular assemblies, Chávez was building a conspiratorial movement in the army. But he and other young soldiers were also in close contact with the revolutionary

---

5   Marx, *Civil War in France*, 633.

underground, and in particular with a figure who would be even more important for the form that the Venezuelan communes would take: the guerrilla commander Kléber Ramírez Rojas. In fact, when Chávez and others were planning their 1992 coup against the corrupt and violent two-party system, Kléber was drafting the founding documents for a new political system to be established if the coup were successful. The goal of the conspiracy, according to these documents, was not simply to seize the state but to immediately replace it with something very different, which Kléber called a "commoner state," and which Chávez would which later call the "communal state."[6]

For Kléber, a veteran of the armed struggle, who was influenced not only by European Marxism but also by the Venezuelan struggle against slavery and colonialism, this new alternative state was in fact no state at all. Instead, building communal power meant dissolving political power into the community itself; it meant a "broadening of democracy in which the communities will assume the fundamental powers of the state." This was not mere "decentralization," however, the buzzword of choice for the neoliberal reformers of the 1990s, who sought to reduce the role of the state to benefit not the community but capital. The communal alternative Kléber and Chávez envisioned was never about decentralizing power but organizing power in the barrios and the country from the bottom up.

_____

6   These and other quotations are from Kléber Ramírez Rojas, *Historia documental del 4 de febrero* (Caracas: El Perro y la Rana, 2006).

While a commoner state would thus be no state at all, it would nevertheless involve thousands upon thousands of directly democratic neighborhood councils, through which Venezuelans would increasingly take control over their own lives. They would elect their own political delegates and police forces; they would decide what to produce and for whom. Everyday people would be constantly involved in managing their local communities, and institutions would no longer stand above and apart from the people. This kind of organization was already emerging in the barrio assemblies that sprouted up around the time of the Caracazo, but Kléber saw a danger in these dispersed assemblies, with their celebrations of horizontal democracy and local autonomy. Communal power, he argued, could not remain dispersed; it needed to unify into a broad horizon for national struggle, becoming in the process a power, an alternative.

Instead of the state *over* the people, a communal power would instead embody a dynamic relationship *between* institutions and the people that Kléber would describe—provocatively and paradoxically—as a "government of popular insurgency." This was the vision, but the 1992 coup failed, Chávez and others were jailed, and the horizon of the commune dipped once again out of sight, only to reemerge later. From prison, Chávez began to expand on these ideas to theorize the transition toward a new form of political power in Venezuela. The young soldier placed a particular emphasis on the need to build a radically reorganized, "polycentric" system of participatory power that would, in the young Chávez's words, "be very near to the territory of utopia."

These two words—territory and utopia—are essential for grasping the communes today.

When Chávez began his "Golpe de Timón" address twenty years later, he did so holding a thick copy of István Mészáros's *Beyond Capital* in his hand. Like Kléber Ramírez, Mészáros—a Hungarian Marxist—had a major impact on Chávez's own understanding of the role of communes in the transition toward a socialist society. In particular, Mészáros had foregrounded the need for socialism to be radically democratic, even going so far as to argue that participatory self-management is the "yardstick" by which progress toward socialism can be measured. But while Chávez was citing Mészáros as an authority and inspiration, it was Chávez himself who had, in part, inspired Mészáros's own emphasis on participatory, radical democracy.[7]

So where *is* the commune? When Chávez asked the question in 2012, the future of this ambitious communal project was far from certain. But since then—in large part due to the momentum provided by his "Golpe de Timón" speech—the communal project has advanced by leaps and bounds. After Chávez died on March 5, 2013, the newly elected president, Nicolás Maduro, named Reinaldo Iturriza commune minister. A radical with deep roots in barrio and youth movements, and with a militant emphasis on popular participation and culture, Iturriza oversaw the revitalization of Chávez's vision

7 István Mészáros, *Beyond Capital: Towards a Theory of Transition* (New York: Monthly Review Press, 2010), 739. Chávez's words above are in fact quoted by Mészáros (711).

and the dramatic expansion of the communes. From a small handful registered between 2010 and 2013, there were soon dozens, then hundreds, then more than a thousand communes, and Maduro was speaking openly of the need to "demolish the bourgeois state." As I write this, the real-time tally of registered communes on the ministry's website reads 1,546, in addition to more than 45,000 communal councils, and thousands of EPSs already registered by 2013.

In a major step forward, 2014 saw the communes begin to stretch their authority upward, consolidating an integrated national structure. Communes now elect delegates to state-level confederations with their own parliaments, which in turn send delegates to a national presidential council that interfaces directly with Maduro. While some—especially outside Venezuela—might interpret such a direct connection to the president as reinforcing the centralized authority of the president himself, many organizers reject this view. For national commune organizer Gerardo Rojas, who travels the country facilitating the establishment and consolidation of the communes, the presidential council represents a meeting among equals: the confederated force of communal power and a president who, up to this point at least, has supported the communes.

While formally working for the government—"until they fire me," he chuckles—Rojas nevertheless has a flexible and open-ended vision of the construction of this communal power. When I ask him whether the communes have been a success or failure, whether we are winning or losing, he rightly scoffs at the naivety of the question. The project is advancing, he insists, although his words are measured. Do some communes function better and enjoy a higher degree of participation than others? Do some communes produce more than others? Yes, some produce more material goods—corn, plantains, coffee, sugar—while others, as we will see in later chapters, don't produce much of anything at all. But these too are spaces in which residents are attempting to build a new culture and a new form of radically democratic self-government that, according to Rojas, "exists and is tangible in many parts of the country right now."

It would be a mistake, Rojas insists, to define the commune in too rigid a way, to straitjacket it from above when its ultimate form needs to be determined by the grassroots participation of millions from below. He insists that, if anything, the commune is best understood as a sort of revolutionary myth that, rather than prescribing a fixed form, can instead help to mobilize the masses to do the impossible and create something altogether new. If Marx once described the commune as a "sphinx so tantalizing to the bourgeois mind," contemporary Venezuela shows that it can be equally tantalizing to those who see their own future in it.

Such revolutionary myths are more urgently necessary now than ever before, and the years since Chávez's death have been trying times for Venezuelan revolutionaries. Chávez's death coincided with a collapse in global oil prices drastic enough to throw the stability of the Bolivarian process into question and to embolden its opponents. Anti-Chavista forces have seized upon the economic crisis—which has seen dramatic inflation and shortages of basic goods— to rally disaffected voters, handing the Chavistas an unprecedented defeat in the December 2015 National Assembly elections. But despite political and economic crisis looming from above, grassroots organizers have pressed ahead to build an ambitious communal alternative from below.

The communal project today unifies and condenses the revolutionary energy of the Venezuelan grassroots—it is the project of projects, coalescing the aspirations of many different grassroots sectors and their struggles. In the process, the communes embody both the present and the future of the Bolivarian process: with the commune, so goes the Revolution. But to stand at the forefront of historical motion is to occupy an uneasy and unstable position, pressing forward with no blueprints to consult, no banisters on which to lean, neither comfortably cradled by the dialectical oppositions of the present nor pulled along in their wake.

From such a position, nothing is guaranteed. If anything, the opposite is the case: the odds are never in our favor. This much is clear today amid the persistence of corruption and bureaucracy, the mounting economic crisis, and the continued aggression by ferocious enemies in Venezuela and beyond. "We are in the worst moment of the Bolivarian Revolution," Rojas confesses with a sort of exasperated pride, "but *chamo* . . . the communes, that's where the vitality is."

2

THE BARRIOS AND THE STRUGGLE FOR URBAN SPACE

In Caracas, the rich have felt surrounded for decades. And they are surrounded—never more so than today. Stand on the rooftop of any building, and you have an almost 360-degree view of the poor barrios that ring the city's hilltops, broken only by the mountainous El Ávila National Park to the north, known since 2011 by its indigenous name, Waraira Repano. These mountains, which once sheltered the city from Caribbean pirates, today shelter the rich from a similarly fearsome threat—the poor—with the wealthiest enclaves of the city tucked just south of the national park where barrio settlements are prohibited. Absent the kind of white exodus that saw elites abandon urban centers in the United States, their Venezuelan counterparts often dug in. Building checkpoints and higher walls, paying for guards and new security systems, they refused to leave.

The borders are sharp. Wealthy eastern Caracas ends abruptly where the Francisco Fajardo Highway swings suddenly northward toward the mountains. As the city expanded eastward, poor migrants took over this area, building ramshackle housing where an old sugarcane plantation once stood. But starting in the 1960s, a series of governments criminalized these settlements of the poor before eventually evicting them, tearing out their fresh roots and pushing their residents further east to build the highway and, in the refuge that this asphalt barrier provided from the poor, to build modern apartment blocks as well. Today, the streets are cleanly gridded and interspersed with green spaces, their crisp ninety-degree angles projected vertically in the highrises that line them.

Across the highway, however, is a dense tangle of unmarked streets, paths, and walkways, and of hundreds of thousands of self-constructed homes stacked one on top of the other. This is Petare, the largest and most dangerous slum in all Venezuela, if not all Latin America. After Chávez was elected, the opposition soon accused him of dividing the country with his aggressive rhetoric in defense of the poor and against the oligarchs. In response, Chavistas began to circulate a meme consisting of an image of the Fajardo Highway—an asphalt ribbon dividing rich from poor—with the incredulous caption: "It was Chávez who divided us?" The message is clear: the division was there long before Chávez helped to reveal it.

This division is clear even in language. At first, the rich called the barrio residents *marginals*, and the term was certainly an accurate description of the segregation they suffered. Lured to the capital by the promise of access to oil wealth, newcomers were instead confined to the outskirts of the cities. It was on the unstable terrain of the hills surrounding Caracas that they erected first cardboard, then tin, and finally cement homes as their informal settlements gained a degree of permanence. These were never truly permanent, however: lacking a stable foundation—legal or geological—their residents were often forcibly displaced through government evictions, or by the precarious terrain itself betraying them in unpredictable mudslides, periodic torrents of mud, flesh, and bone.

Despite being labeled as marginal, however, the residents of the shantytowns were in fact central to the circulatory system of the capital. These were the people who cooked for the rich, cleaned their homes, cared for their children, parked their cars, and guarded their buildings and belongings. Wealthy Venezuelans thus suffered the permanent contradiction of colonial and capitalist elites alike: they were dependent upon the labor of people they were desperate to avoid at all costs. In the early 1980s, a regional debt crisis across Latin America coincided with a sharp drop in oil prices to throw the Venezuelan economy into a tailspin. Armed revolutionary movements—heirs of the 1960s guerrilla struggle but long isolated from poor communities—capitalized on discontent in the barrios over increasing drug violence and the need for running water, electricity, schools, and health care.

The increasingly corrupt and unresponsive Venezuelan two-party system—unable and unwilling to provide for the poorest—responded to rebellion with massacre, killing twenty-three guerrillas in Cantaura in 1982, nine student organizers in Yumare in 1986, and fourteen unarmed fishermen in El Amparo in 1988. But no massacre was more devastating than the concluding act of the 1989 Caracazo, provoked by then-president Carlos Andrés Pérez's neoliberal reform package. During the Caracazo, the urban poor of Venezuela's barrios looted everything from basic goods to imported whiskey. But most importantly, they took over the city, broke the bounds of informal segregation, and entered zones previously reserved for the rich.

Never before had the space of Venezuela's wealthy, white elites been breached so suddenly and so devastatingly by the poor. In response, the polite rhetoric of the rich gave way to open expressions of racism and class hatred that mixed together in anxious denunciations of the rabble, the mob, and the hordes. To this day, nothing provokes the panic of the wealthy like a poor-looking motorcyclist, or *motorizado*, unpredictably crossing the bounds of this informally segregated landscape. Many wealthy *caraqueños* still speak of the Caracazo as the day when, in a peculiarly dehumanizing phrase, "the hills came down"—the poor entered the city not as individuals seeking poorly paid work, but as a collective seeking equality. But when the state killed hundreds, even thousands, in the same barrios it had marginalized for so long, it set into motion revolutionary social movements and a military conspiracy that would eventually see Hugo Chávez thrown into the seat of power.

The shock and fear that the Caracazo inspired in elites led to "progressive" urban reforms like the Organic Law for Municipal Government, which claimed that decentralizing the city into autonomous municipalities would lead to better governance. While the law—conceived prior to but hastily approved after the Caracazo—was presented as a solution to the social exclusion that had created the rebellion, in reality, it only made things worse. Within two years, new municipalities in the wealthiest part of the capital had effectively seceded, claiming autonomy from city government, electing their own mayors, and—crucially—establishing their own police forces.

Already wealthier than much of the urban area, these new municipalities—and in particular the sheltered central business district of Chacao—used their newfound autonomy to drain even more revenue away from the traditional city center, no longer the center of the capital's wealth. Deploying their enhanced policing powers to cleanse neighborhoods of marginal populations, these rich enclaves trumpeted their safety in contrast to other, less fortified areas. The same year Chávez was elected, Chacao outlawed the informal street vendors who make up a considerable segment of the city's workforce; faithful to its brand, the municipality has more recently declared its intention to become Venezuela's first "graffiti-free" zone.

Urban decentralization was seen as a cure-all by a ruling class that was utterly oblivious to just how deep the shit had gotten. As it turned out, though, the urban poor were no anomaly, but living, breathing symptoms of the system itself, the natural products of a class of elites that lacked then—as it lacks today—any coherent alternative for Venezuela's economic and social development. Alongside this decentralization of political power and policing in Caracas, the echoes of the Caracazo played out in a multitude of large- and small-scale changes that built fear into the very architecture of the city. Electric fences, barbed wire, gated communities, and even residential checkpoints quickly became the norm. In the words of the poet François Migeot:

> In their housing developments
> they placed first, broken bottles on top of their walls,
> then, barriers and armed guards,
> barbed wire, bars, attack dogs,
> and now, triple-wired electric fences
> like a Nazi camp . . . [but]
> the concentration camp is the street,
> the barrio hills and poverty,
> the dust and the junk,
> where they live, God willing.[1]

As architecture became increasingly militarized, so too did policing. Attention shifted from individual suspects to entire populations, identified through a combination of skin color and perceived "marginality." Caracas increasingly reflected Frantz Fanon's description of colonial Algeria as a Manichaean world, a "compartmentalized world . . . divided in two" and "inhabited by different species."[2]

~

---

1   François Migeot, *Andante con apuro* (Caracas: El Perro y la Rana, 2006).

2   Frantz Fanon, *The Wretched of the Earth*, trans. R Philcox (New York: Grove Press, 2004 [1961]), 5–6.

For white elites who rarely saw Afro- and indigenous Venezuelans on television, much less in the seat of power, Hugo Chávez's 1998 election was no less violent than his failed 1992 coup. Chávez's early political proposals were moderate, carefully avoiding the language of class combat and racial reparation, and while this won him some middle-class support, many hated him from day one. His dark face and indigenous features marked him as a usurper to the throne that had always been theirs alone. But the more stubbornly these wealthy elites hated him, the more Chávez realized that compromising with them was impossible—and the more radical he became.

In 2001, Chávez passed by decree a radical Land Law that facilitated the expropriation of idle land in the countryside; this was followed in early 2002 by a similar decree for urban areas allowing poor residents who had built their own homes on unoccupied barrio land to claim that land as their own. This urban land decree did not simply announce urban land distribution from above, however. It empowered radical grassroots movements to make this promise a reality themselves. The first step was to legally enshrine what are called urban land committees (CTUs), one of the first tools for popular participation to emerge in the Bolivarian process. The CTUs were essentially a way for barrio residents to gain formal ownership over land they had occupied and improved, even when it had once legally belonged to someone else.

Crucially, the CTUs did so by making *collective* organizing a precondition to *individual* ownership—to make a land claim, residents needed to first organize their community into a CTU. In the process, it was hoped that the CTUs would help avoid the common tendency for social demands for land to wind up simply reinforcing capitalist private property. By 2016, more than 650,000 titles to urban land had been granted through the CTUs, benefiting more than a million families.[3] Alongside other mechanisms like the technical water tables—which similarly bring neighbors together to collectively manage local access to clean water—and more recently the communal councils and communes themselves, the CTUs form part of a broad constellation of participatory institutions where the constituted power of the state meets the constituent power of the grassroots.

Once established, these CTUs provided even more space for grassroots movements to occupy in order to leverage more radical change. This includes the more daring tactics of the Movimiento de Pobladores (Squatters' Movement), which links the CTUs with tenants' networks, building custodians and caretakers, and "pioneer camps" that engage in land occupations. Much like Brazil's Landless and Homeless Workers' Movements, the Squatters' Movement uses direct action tactics, seizing urban land first before constructing self-managed housing, and only then demanding legal title. Such controversial tactics—which the opposition decries as "invasions"— also push the envelope of mainstream Chavismo, with many government officials considering them too

---

3   "Más de 800 familias fueron beneficiadas con la entrega de títulos de tierras urbana," *Noticias24*, February 25, 2016, noticias24.com.

provocative and even anarchic. But the Squatters' Movement sees such tactics as an essential part of what they consider to be a war against the "urban *latifundistas*," a term that evokes the large landholders more often associated with the countryside. And despite their controversial approach, the Squatters' Movement found a powerful ally in Chávez himself, who eventually endorsed the movement and the right to occupy vacant urban land.

More than seven years ago, the Squatters' Movement helped to organize families left homeless by landslides to take over an empty office building overlooking Sabana Grande Boulevard, the bustling heart of the city's commercial center. Today, ninety-eight families live here on an entirely collective and self-managed basis, sharing the work of constructing, maintaining, and cleaning the apartments and the building. All decisions are made collectively in an assembly. From the looks of the walls, a patchwork of partially exposed pipes and wires, and holes punched for repairs and never covered up, the entire process is radically improvisational. In the hallway, a chart itemizes shared costs for security and water, as well as a rotating cleaning schedule for the common spaces.

Members of the Squatters' Movement see themselves explicitly as contributing to a reverse boomerang swing against the segregation of the city. They insist that they are actually reclaiming urban space at the center of the city from the forces of financial capital that had driven out the poor. When I visited, organizers from the Squatters' Movement and residents were testing a radio transmitter, 93.7 FM, that they hoped would reach the entire city from a small studio here. Despite the opposition's misinformation about press censorship, community media has flourished since Chávez was elected, with the exception of those two days in 2002 when the opposition took power and targeted grassroots media directly.

With the support of experienced technicians from the National Community Media Association (ANMCLA), organizers soldered the necessary wires into place and tested the radio transmitter. The equipment needed a cool space, and a discussion ensued about how best to vent a small portable air conditioner. By the end, yet another hole punched in a wall stood as evidence of a successful experiment in democratic self-management. Out on the balcony, amid hundreds of bags of cement, plaster, and other supplies, organizers huddled around a radio receiver: the test was a success, and the radio station launched later that week.

Overlooking the very center of one of the most populated areas of Caracas from within what could only be described as a vertical commune, bags of cement stacked nearby and pipes and tubes of all shapes and sizes underfoot, a young organizer confessed to me: "I was never politically involved before. I never even went to our communal council." But that all changed when his family home was destroyed in a landslide, and he and his former neighbors began to organize to demand he right to housing. From that specific struggle, he explained, his political consciousness evolved by leaps and bounds, and that small group of neighbors eventually seized this building directly before pressuring the government to expropriate it.

This return of the poor to the heart of the metropolis raises for many the fearful memory of that not-so-distant rebellion more than twenty-five years ago, the Caracazo. The reaction of some wealthy elites has been one of violent panic, but it isn't just squatters who evoke this fear. In the last fifteen years, the government has compensated for the desperate shortage of urban housing, especially in Caracas, with ambitious programs like the Misión Vivienda (Housing Mission), which has built more than a million low-income housing units since 2011, with a stated goal of more than 2 million by 2018. These towering red-and-white apartment blocks were originally relegated to less desirable and even "marginal" locations. But more recently, they have begun to spring up in in the wealthier central zones of Caracas as well, provoking opposition protests in response.[4]

In the run-up to Nicolás Maduro's election in April 2013, opposition marchers regularly invaded the government housing projects of Misión Vivienda. Later, after Maduro was elected, defeated opposition candidate Henrique Capriles urged his followers to "unload their fury" in the streets, and some chose to vent their rage in a mob attack on the La Limonera Commune in the opposition stronghold of Baruta,

---

4   In early 2016, the Venezuelan Supreme Court blocked an attempt by the opposition-controlled National Assembly to convert Misión Vivienda apartments into individually held property that could be resold on the private market.

where Capriles was once mayor. More than two thousand families had come to live here in hostile territory, establishing a communal farm and carpentry workshop. One of the communal carpenters, José Luis Ponce, was killed alongside Rosiris Reyes—both were shot when opposition protesters besieged the local Cuban-staffed health clinic. According to a journalist investigating the scene, this was a "social cleansing"—a term that evokes Colombian paramilitary violence—since the two were killed for nothing more than the crime of daring to move into public housing.

Venezuelan elites clearly understand that "dignified housing" means the poor returning to the heart of the city from which they had been so systematically cleansed. It was thus no coincidence that these right-wing attacks would target public housing projects, just as it was no coincidence when—during the 2014 youth protests I discuss in the next chapter—opposition mobs attacked and burned the housing program's headquarters in Chacao. Nor was it any coincidence when an abandoned skyscraper known as the Tower of David became a lightning rod for elite fears when it was taken over by the poor.

The third-tallest building in all Venezuela, the Tower of David was abandoned before completion amid the financial crisis of the 1990s. More than a decade later, in 2007, displaced families spontaneously occupied the tower, transforming it into a massive, self-managed, vertical barrio. While this was not a commune, strictly speaking—the tower was not run democratically—it was nevertheless an undeniable expression of popular dignity and legitimate demands for housing. But rather than see the abandoned building for what it was

(the crisis of the old) and the occupation for what it represented (the creativity of the new), the Tower of David was
somehow transformed into its opposite: a fearful symbol of
the failures of the Bolivarian Revolution.[5]

In early 2012, a short amateur video titled *City of Goodbyes*
quickly went viral, providing a direct glimpse into the mind-
set of young elites tempted to abandon the homeland for
more northern comforts. In the film, between art-student
experiments with depth of field and musical interludes,
hip-looking twentysomethings in posh apartments and lush
suburban retreats tell of how every weekend brings another
goodbye party as more and more of their friends abandon
Venezuela. The film, which even one opposition blogger at
Caracas Chronicles described as "dismally devoid of
self-awareness," oozes the kind of privilege one might expect
from "a bunch of aggressively spoiled rich white kids sitting
around feeling sorry for themselves."[6] The film reflects the
utter decadence of a class that no longer enjoys privileged
access to government jobs and has instead been forced to rely
on the stunted private sector, itself clinging parasitically to
the bloated petro-state.

City of Goodbyes was roundly mocked by Chavistas and
became fodder for dozens of memes, but were this simply the

---

5 As just one breathtakingly awful example of demonizing the poor
residents of the tower while blaming the Venezuelan government for a problem it didn't create, see Jon Lee Anderson, "Slumlord," *New Yorker*, January
28, 2013.

6 The post, by Francisco Toro, has since been deleted.

tragicomic expression of a displaced elite, we could welcome their departure and be done with it, no tears shed but in laughter (after all, more people move to Venezuela than abandon it). But as it turns out, this repressed desire to escape would return with a vengeance in the middle-class rage vented during the 2014 protests. In the film, a young woman, Raquel Abend van Dalen, who has since abandoned Venezuela for the New York literary scene, muses that "Caracas would be so perfect without the people"—a thinly veiled wish for the poor to return to obscurity, or worse. Another wonders aloud "how this whole situation will end."

More important, and more dangerous for the future of the Bolivarian Revolution, are the class conflicts emerging within its ranks, which can even mimic the fearful vilification of the barrio poor by the rich. Many political leaders view the urban poor with contempt, as passive recipients of social welfare programs rather than as active participants in recent history. "What the hell is that?" wonders Reinaldo Iturriza. "The people won this and have defended it, and defended Chávez when they put him back in power after he was overthrown in April 2002."

This class struggle within Chavismo has cultural implications that threaten to deepen the divide between political leaders and barrio youth. Iturriza himself scandalized many Chavistas when, after transitioning from commune minister to culture minister, he declared an appreciation for reggaetón music, wildly popular among poor Venezuelans. Reggaetón's salacious lyrics—not to mention the provocative dance styles that accompany it—provoked a moral panic in Puerto Rico in the 1990s. A similar moralism is common today even among critically minded revolutionaries, for whom the entire genre is too apolitical and blatantly sexist and commercial.

Meanwhile, unusual depictions of Chávez began to appear in murals painted throughout the sprawling barrios of Petare. They showed Chávez rapping in an oversized hoodie, Chávez sporting the dark sunglasses of a reggaetón singer, and a Chávez closer to reality, playing an accordion befitting the *llanero* music of his native Barinas. There was Chávez popping a wheelie on a motorcycle, a muscular boxing Chávez delivering a knockout punch, a tattooed Chávez with arms crossed, and another with an ornately sculpted haircut characteristic of young men in the barrios, with the caption: "Chávez has style."

A single slogan brought all these images together: "*Chávez es otro beta.*" The murals were the work of the Otro Beta movement, and everything is in the name: in barrio slang, the *beta* is the main hustle, be it drugs, gangs, or both. By declaring Chávez *otro beta*, these young organizers were attempting to communicate that the Revolution was another hustle to be undertaken, another gang to join. They sought to show that barrio culture itself—which is rooted in a struggle against all odds—had plenty of revolutionary potential that needed only to be redirected. For these organizers, moreover, engaging revolutionary culture is a two-way street, the goal of which is to politicize barrio youth *and* to radicalize Chavismo by provoking a cultural revolution in the Revolution.

Whereas more official Chavista organizations often attempt to politicize new recruits by sitting them down and lecturing at them, Otro Beta militant Gabriela Henríquez explained that "We do it differently," allowing barrio youth to participate on their own terms, without renouncing who they are or where they come from. To this end, organizers participate not only in graffiti campaigns but also in cultural events and sports tournaments, all the while adapting to the terrain they seek to organize. Rather than dismiss hip-hop culture out of hand, they infuse it with a participatory spirit, organizing rap concerts but also training barrio youth in music production and event management in the process.

When Otro Beta recently organized an inter-barrio sports tournament, moreover, they took their lead from those on the ground. The tournament consisted of not only basketball, but also *pelotica de goma*—an urban sport if ever there was one, a sort of handball played in the streets with nothing but fists and a rubber ball. The tournament also included the death-defying motorcycle tricks that have become a cultural staple of barrio life. More recently, Otro Beta launched an initiative, with the support of Iturriza's culture ministry, whose name says it all: "Culture Is the Barrio." Needless to say, all of this is a disgrace for those well-heeled Chavistas who reproduce, however naturally and unconsciously, the class prejudices of the old system.

The organizers from Otro Beta insist that they, too, are building the commune. Unlike most others, they are doing so specifically in the barrios, Petare in particular. This makes their work risky—Petare is notoriously dangerous, and they have suffered shootings and assassinations at their events, and are currently working on establishing cease-fires between local gangs. It also means that they work on a terrain that is as unstable politically as it is geologically, and that their effort to organize "not the ones already wearing red" but those the Bolivarian process still excludes is a constant and uphill struggle.

As the entire history of the Boliviarian process makes clear enough, however, the poorest of the poor often possess an embryonic revolutionary consciousness. Even some gang members and *malandros*, or delinquents, act on an ethics grounded in the everyday reality of class inequality: robbing in rich neighborhoods but not their own neighbors. This instinctual class consciousness can often lead to political clarity. One Otro Beta organizer in Petare explained to me how, during the 2014 opposition protests, "the delinquents were taking it upon themselves to dismantle the roadblocks. They may be criminals, but they're also Chavistas, and they're politically clear about that." When I asked about the impact of their organizing efforts in Petare, organizers insisted that they have seen both increased support for the Revolution and a decrease in violence between local gangs.

Across the city, high in the barrio of Antímano, which dramatically overlooks all of Caracas, it is clear that the cultural struggle is indeed an uphill one—no pun intended. This too is a hotbed of gang activity with a long history of violent territorial clashes over control of the drug trade. Both despite and because of this history, the line between revolutionaries and so-called delinquents here is visceral. But rather than attempting to break down the distinction and integrate barrio youth into Chavismo, some members of the José Félix Ribas Commune participate actively in making that line sharper, distinguishing *we* the commune from *they* the dangerous criminals.

There are both push and pull factors at play. Many young people are unlikely to participate in political organizing without sustained institutional support, and sitting around debating local infrastructure projects is not what most teenagers consider a good time. But when politicized Chavistas distinguish "good" revolutionaries from "bad" delinquents, they can provide fodder for the idea that the latter need to be eliminated by the police. And if the question becomes one of the communes versus the barrio youth, reproducing a deep distrust of the poor among the poor themselves that feeds into the same kind of heavy-handed policing that characterized the old political system, Chavista identity will have suffered a fatal blow.[7]

Latent in this question is another question that is even more complex: What happens to a movement of the poor when the people are no longer poor? As poverty declined dramatically, and as health and education became widely accessible, life in the barrios changed. As a result, while many remain poor, others have lost their patience with what they perceive as delinquent culture: No one, so the argument goes, needs to be a criminal today in the way they did in the past,

---

7   In the 2015 anti-crime offensive known as "Operation Free the People," in which hardline policing provided a justification for mass arrests and extrajudicial killing in the barrios, this danger became a reality.

because no one is starving. But the question has never been so simple as socioeconomic status, and to draw the lines too hard will only create a self-fulfilling prophecy in which the poorest of the poor will embrace the negative aspects of barrio life at the expense of the Revolution.

These conflicts, for the radical sociologist and organizer Ociel López, have only sharpened with the "fattening" of the state through oil wealth and the creation of a new Chavista middle class, "with its own interests and new fears." These new fears mimic the very old fears of the wealthy, for whom barrio youth—like the marginals of the past—provoke terror and panic. Chavismo, in other words, might just be creating its own gravediggers—and if the Revolution "loses influence in the barrios" where it began, it may just lose everything.[8]

For now, though, the petrified and segregated geography of Caracas and other cities is beginning to show signs of cracking. The poorest of the poor, those once confined to the peripheral slums surrounding Venezuelan cities, have begun to take matters into their own hands, leveraging the government to reclaim urban space and make it their own. But the rich rarely go quietly without a fight, and in 2014 they would find an opportunity to vent their furious rage.

---

8 Ociel Alí López, *¡Dale Más Gasolina! Chavismo, Sifrinismo y Burocracia* (Caracas: Fundación Casa Nacional de las Letras Andrés Bello), 109, 111.

3
COUNTERREVOLUTION

Ours is increasingly an age of riots and rebellions, of radical self-creation in the streets: from London to Paris, the Arab Spring to Occupy, and more recently, the explosive fury of Ferguson and Baltimore. We are justifiably excited by the heat of the crowd; our collective pulse may even rise at the sight of masks, broken glass, and flames, because for so long these have represented the shards of the old world through which shines the glint of the new. Indeed, the global rebelliousness of the present owes much to the revolt—and repression—that marked Venezuela's and Latin America's own awakening from the neoliberal nightmare.

But while the new Venezuela was born of popular insurrection in the 1989 Caracazo, recent years have made perfectly clear that not every fire is an omen of liberation, and not every mask conceals a comrade. (This much should have been perfectly clear when *Time* named the masked protester its 2011 person of the year.) To assume otherwise is to mistake form for content and image for reality. In this sense, the early months of 2014 were a wakeup call not only to Venezuela but also to a global left that is often more focused on the cataclysmic spectacle and militant posture than on the underlying political dynamics at play.

When the Venezuelan right took to the streets under the guise of spontaneous popular resistance to an authoritarian regime, it had patiently studied the tools, imagery, and social media techniques more often associated with progressive or leftist causes. Protesters took strategically to Twitter, with desperate hashtags like #SOSVenezuela and #PrayForVenezuela that earned them naive retweets from celebrities like Cher and Madonna. Their overarching goal was to integrate their own protests seamlessly into the narrative of global revolt and resistance. But if the current global wave of rebellion erupted in opposition to neoliberalism and austerity measures, seeking instead to build participatory democratic institutions from Tahrir Square to Zuccotti Park, many of those who took to the streets in Venezuela had far different objectives.

The 2014 protests—known among Chavistas as the *guarimbas* for the treacherous barricades they erected—had far more to do with returning to a neoliberal past than with charting a revolutionary future. The hashtag that represented the aims of these middle-class Twitter warriors most honestly was the original one—#LaSalida, "the exit"—pointing toward the goal of regime change at all costs. The way that the protesters appropriated the symbols of the left was no accident, moreover, but instead involved global networks of foundations and NGOs that have gradually co-opted the tools of the left—strategic nonviolence, street protest, and social media—fusing these instead with a young, new Latin American right wing.

On the surface of things, the sudden outbreak of nationwide protests in February 2014 could be seen as simply the next step in a wave of unrelenting aggression against Nicolás Maduro that began even before he was elected to succeed Chávez. Immediately after Maduro's narrow victory in April 2013, opposition candidate Henrique Capriles urged his followers to "unload their fury" in the streets. The result was at least eleven dead—mostly celebrating Chavistas—with arson attacks on local Socialist Party (PSUV) headquarters, the home of the electoral council president, and numerous social service providers. These notably included Venezuela's Cuban-staffed health clinics for the poor, thirty-five of which were attacked after opposition journalist Nelson Bocaranda tweeted the bogus claim that they were hiding ballot boxes to his more than one million followers.[1]

But there were deeper dynamics at play. By late 2013, Capriles seemed to have learned the one lesson that most of the Venezuelan opposition could not grasp: that radical street action calling for the overthrow of an elected government might satisfy the far right, but it would never attract a majority. Having won over some 600,000 Chavista voters in 2013 by softening his rhetoric and promising not to eliminate the

    1   "Twitter de Nelson Bocaranda desata violencia contra CDI y médicos cubanos," *Correo del Orinoco*, April 16, 2013, http://www.correodelorinoco.gob.ve/politica/twitter-nelson-bocaranda-desata-violencia-contra-cdi-y-medicos-cubanos/.

popular social programs Chávez instituted, Capriles now realized that the only path to victory was through the slow political work of winning over millions more. But when municipal elections in December 2013 saw the Chavistas stretch their lead to nearly 10 percentage points—compared to the 1.5 percent margin of victory earlier that same year—the opposition was at an impasse.

They had nearly won their first national election in two decades, only to be immediately trounced on the local level. Facing the prospect of long-term base-building political work for elections they might never actually win, the most impatient sectors of the far right rejected Capriles's long-term electoral strategy and opted instead for the short-term strategy of the streets. At their head stood the photogenic firebrands of the Venezuelan opposition, Leopoldo López and María Corina Machado—too white, too elite, and too controversial to win over many Chavista voters themselves (Machado is still widely reviled for her smiling 2005 photo-op with George W. Bush at the White House). In other words, the #SOSVenezuela protests emerged not out of the strength and unity of the Venezuelan opposition, but out of a deep division between those committed to taking the democratic route and those more than willing to use other means.

For those who still insist that these were spontaneous protests, the timeline should prove embarrassing enough. On January 23, 2014, more than a full week before the so-called spontaneous student protests erupted, López and Machado called publicly for Maduro's ouster ("La Salida") through a

strategy of "igniting the streets with struggle."[2] When the
protests then broke out in the opposition stronghold of
Táchira—tucked along the Colombian border in Venezuela's
Andean region and rife with paramilitary activity—a small
group of masked opposition protesters attacked the house of
Chavista governor José Vielma Mora, leading to some arrests.
With admirable indifference to the facts, rumors quickly circu-
lated across the country and in the international media: the
Venezuelan government was repressing the people. Protests
were called nationwide according to a quickly crafted narrative about violent crime and economic shortages, with little
mention of the opposition's public call to oust the
government.

The ensuing struggle was carried out above all on
Twitter, where opposition activists quickly gained an
unprecedented degree of international attention, indeed far
more than their small numbers warranted. The sinister face
of social media was on full display. Misrepresentations,
manipulations, exaggerations, and outright lies were
disseminated in a flash. Images of police brutality against
students in Chile and Brazil, Indonesia and Singapore, even
the bodies of dead Syrians in Aleppo were all recycled as
proof of Maduro's repressive nature. This sensationalism
explains in part the effectiveness of the opposition's social
media strategy. The mainstream media were not immune:
In the earlier wave of protests following Maduro's election,

---

2   "López y Machado llaman a 'prender las calles de lucha,'" *El Diario de
Caracas*, January 23, 2014, diariodecaracas.com. The entire press conference
can be viewed here: youtube.com/watch?v=IwTrta9T23Q.

the Venezuela correspondent for the Spanish newspaper *ABC* published an article denouncing the government's "fascism" that featured a well-known image of an unknown, semiclothed woman being dragged by Egyptian police.[3] During the 2014 protests, media outlets were similarly quick to tweet and retweet misleading images. As soon as one image, one imaginary event, could be debunked—for example, an image of police clearly bearing the obsolete insignia of the Metropolitan Police, disbanded years earlier—a dozen more had taken its place. In a country as polarized as Venezuela, both supporters and opponents of the government rarely need hard proof to believe what they are already convinced is the truth.

For those who insist that the protests were nonviolent, the facts again betray the narrative, which began to crumble almost immediately. When the smoke cleared months later, there were forty-three dead. While some who protested did so peacefully, the predominant narrative of government repression implies a one-sided death count. In reality, however, the deaths that ensued were evenly distributed among Chavistas, opposition members, bystanders, and security officials. Some were shot dead by protesters for simply crossing barricades to get to work; several police and military officials were killed by sniper fire raining down from rooftops near opposition barricades. More damaging still for the opposition media narrative were the openly violent tendencies of many protesters who

---

3 "La corresponsal de *ABC* en Venezuela ilustra el 'fascismo puro y ma-duro' con una foto de Egipto," *El Diario*, April 19, 2013, eldiario.es.

didn't even bother to toe the media line, like those in the opposition hotbed of Táchira who, brandishing a variety of homemade weapons, told the *New York Times*, "We're not peaceful here."[4] In these areas, bystanders and even journalists were often attacked, threatened, robbed, and charged a toll to cross the barricades.

And then there was the biggest embarrassment of all: the retired general Ángel Vivas, who tweeted the suggestion that wires be hung across streets "to neutralize the criminal motorcycle hordes" associated with Chavismo. When youth on the barricades took up this suggestion, a twenty-nine-year-old supermarket worker was decapitated and a thirty-seven-year-old woman traveling on a motorcycle with her child died in a crash after colliding with a wire. An arrest order was issued for Vivas, but when police arrived the next day, the retired general had barricaded himself in his home, appearing on his balcony with a bulletproof vest and automatic rifle to denounce a Cuban takeover of the country in the most paranoid of terms. True to form, CNN en Español lavished attention on this figure who would have been denounced as a fringe lunatic anywhere else in the world, even sending a correspondent to Vivas's home for an extensive interview. (To this day, the "repressive" regime has decided to leave him barricaded in his compound rather than risk a violent conflict).

~

---

4   William Neuman, "Crude Weapons Help Fuel Unrest in Bastion of Venezuelan Opposition," *New York Times*, February 25, 2014.

To insist that the protests were neither spontaneous nor nonviolent is not to dismiss the motivations of some who protested—insecurity and shortages were and remain undeniable challenges in contemporary Venezuela. But, as many pointed out at the time, insecurity and shortages were a problem when Maduro was narrowly elected in April 2013, and were still a problem when the Chavistas won a more sweeping victory in local elections that December. (In fact, when a ten-point list of demands emerged from Táchira early in the protest wave, the demands were purely political—focused on so-called political prisoners and Maduro's resignation; insecurity and shortages did not even appear).

Ultimately, the protests remained demographically middle- and upper-class, and they openly embraced the conservative elites at the head of the Venezuelan opposition. As the historian Alejandro Velasco has shown, Venezuela's barrio poor have a deeply ingrained protest culture that includes this kind of combative street blockade, but when the middle-class opposition took to the streets, the poor didn't support them.[5] Despite bearing the brunt of insecurity and shortages, poor Chavistas and non-Chavistas alike were unwilling to lend their support to what many viewed as an antidemocratic movement that sought to overthrow a government elected by the majority.

Many journalists, like Roberto Lovato, visited the front lines, observing obvious markers of wealth like designer

---

5 Alejandro Velasco, *Barrio Rising: Urban Popular Politics and the Making of Modern Venezuela* (Berkeley: University of California Press, 2015).

shoes and even "well-groomed" designer dogs. Politically, the protesters Lovato interviewed rejected any association with Marxism and anarchism—guiding ideologies for many recent protests elsewhere—instead identifying openly with a pack of opposition leaders drawn from some of Venezuela's wealthiest families. Some even celebrated Venezuela's last dictator, Marcos Pérez Jiménez, who was deposed in 1958. For Lovato, these observations made it perfectly clear that the protests—which he deemed "fauxccupy"—had nothing at all to do with the global upsurge at whose coattails these affluent youths grasped.[6]

The protests instead reflected a shared political culture rooted in the history of Venezuela's dominant classes. Class in Venezuela has never been solely about money, revolving instead around a strange mix of race and class that the radical sociologist Ociel López calls "lineage," an inherited nobility limited to the handful of elite Spanish-descended families from which opposition leaders like Machado, López, and Capriles are drawn. The "cultural ethos" of those elites today is firmly grounded in hatred and criminalization of the poor, whom they often denounce with colorful epithets—calling them "monkeys," "hordes," and "scum"—and all of these phrases made appearances during the 2014 protests.[7] As those protests showed, particularly in Vivas's tweets denouncing

---

6   Roberto Lovato, "Venezuela's Opposition Is United Against Maduro but Internally Divided," *Al Jazeera America*, March 5, 2014; "Fauxccupy: The Selling and Buying of the Venezuelan Opposition," *Latino Rebels*, March 13, 2014.

7   López, *¡Dale Más Gasolina!*, 104, 110.

the Chavista "hordes," this hatred of the poor often encourages violent actions against them.

However, these protests did not begin in the traditional outposts of Venezuela's wealthiest colonial elites but further westward, at the foot of the Andes, in remote Táchira State, where the barricades were most proudly violent and where people identify as *gochos*. While urban elites have historically mocked these Andeans as backward hillbillies, hardworking *gocho* pride has never been fully separable from racial superiority. As Winthrop Wright wrote in his classic account of race in Venezuela, the *gochos* "contrasted their austere way of life with that of the darker-hued lowland Venezuelans, whom they depicted as being descendants of fun-loving and frolicking slave ancestors."[8] Politically conservative, contemptuous of the racially inferior, and boasting a hardnosed work ethic that slides quickly into scorn for the undeserving poor, it is not a stretch to suggest that *gocho* identity shares much with supporters of Donald Trump and the Tea Party in the United States.

When *gocho* pride swelled during the protests, it quickly became clear that this was about more than simply regional identity. As one tweet put it at the time: "The *gochos* are the fucking masters of Venezuela," the implication being that everyone else is their rightful slave.[9] Speaking anonymously during the protests, a descendent of one of Venezuela's most elite families described this feeling of ownership among those burning barricades in the streets, who consider themselves

---

8   Winthrop Wright, *Café con Leche: Race, Class, and National Image in Venezuela* (Austin: University of Texas Press, 1990), 70.

9   See twitter.com/Dj_Army1/status/438060468205129728.

"the *true* Venezuelans defending their neighborhoods from the heavily racialized" Chavistas. A similar superiority complex drove protests nationwide: according to one comrade in the working-class zone of El Valle in southern Caracas, those who manned the burning barricades generally live in the tall, more middle-class apartment blocks along the main avenue, and as a result, they "think they are better than the barrio."

This connection to the land would eventually be their undoing. The protests never managed to transcend the wealthiest areas of the country, reaching only an estimated 19 of 335 municipalities nationwide. When small protests occurred in nonelite neighborhoods—though never in the barrios themselves—the feverish celebration of these exceptions on social media only confirmed the general rule. Before long, even sympathizers did not want their neighborhoods shut down for months on end. The 2014 protesters were—and the Venezuelan opposition remains—prisoners of the segregated urban geography they themselves produced. Despite their failures, however, the protests did significant damage to the Maduro government's global image, and they point toward a dangerous new tendency in which far-right youth movements have wrapped themselves in the language of freedom and democracy, adopting the symbols and tactics of the left by cynically co-opting nonviolent struggle toward brutally violent ends.

This new right has proliferated across the continent, especially where they have been displaced from power by the elections of Rafael Correa in Ecuador, Evo Morales in Bolivia, and Hugo Chávez in Venezuela. In Bolivia, for example, the Santa Cruz Youth Union—characterized by the Worldwide Human Rights Movement as a paramilitary group—led a spate of racist attacks in 2008 during separatist violence in the country's wealthy eastern half-moon region; in Ecuador, the right has recently taken to the streets under the familiar banner of "La Salida"; and Venezuelan youth leaders have played a prominent role in the consolidation of this continent-wide right-wing network. If the street tactics of these groups reek of Colombian-style "social cleansing," in which paramilitary forces execute undesirables simply for being poor, this is no accident either. The central figure in this vast network, the inspiration for and deep pockets of the new Latin American reactionaries, is none other than the former narco-president of Colombia, Álvaro Uribe.

In Venezuela, for example, the writer Luis Britto García alleges that both Capriles and López emerged from a far-right international Catholic organization called Tradition, Family, and Property (*Tradición, Familia y Propiedad*). This "fanatical fascist group," in Britto's words, is secretive, conspiratorial, and radically anticommunist, as the name suggests, drawing inspiration from both Uribe and former Chilean dictator Augusto Pinochet.[10] (Tradition, Family, and Property was even briefly banned in Venezuela in 1984, when then-president Jaime Lusinchi accused it of plotting to assassinate the Pope). While calling such groups in Venezuela and elsewhere "fascist" as Britto does might be imprecise, it is not all that extreme. After

---

10   Roberto Lovato, "Why the Media Are Giving a Free Pass to Venezuela's Neo-Fascist Creeps," *Nation*, April 1, 2014.

all, what else would you call packs of young shock troops of the rich, roaming the streets hunting the poor and dark-skinned, deeply convinced of their own racial and class superiority?

In recent years, moreover, these avowedly violent groups have been trained in nonviolent protest techniques, not because they believe in nonviolence—far from it—but because these tactics work. One prominent example of this dangerous new alliance is the Albert Einstein Institution (AEI), founded by nonviolence guru Gene Sharp. As Eva Golinger has demonstrated, the AEI has received funds from the very same US government institutions as the Venezuelan opposition—the National Endowment for Democracy (NED), International Republican Institute (IRI), and the United States Agency for International Development (USAID)—and has used these funds to train the Venezuelan opposition in a new generation of warfare that would use strategic nonviolence to depose a democratically elected president.[11]

In Venezuela, the 2014 protests were only the third act in this drama of right-wing rebranding. After the failure of the 2002 coup, the Venezuelan opposition was desperate for a new strategy and so invited AEI to Caracas. In early 2004, the Cuban-born exile Robert Alonso boasted of having met with AEI shortly before Venezuela was rocked by the first wave of violent street blockades, a tactic Alonso himself bragged about having invented. So dedicated to nonviolence was Alonso that police soon discovered fifty armed

---

11   Eva Golinger, *Bush vs. Chávez: Washington's War on Venezuela* (New York: Monthly Review, 2007).

Colombian paramilitaries on his estate just south of Caracas, sent with the express purpose of assassinating Hugo Chávez.[12]

It was in the second act of this drama that Venezuela's young right wing, and its students in particular, truly began to shine. According to an analysis published by Stratfor, Venezuelan student leaders traveled to Belgrade in 2005 to meet representatives of the AEI-trained opposition movement Otpor, which had contributed to the overthrow of Slobodan Milošević, before later traveling to Boston to consult directly with Gene Sharp himself.[13] (Like Venezuelan opposition groups, Otpor had received funding from the NED, IRI, and USAID). When these allegedly spontaneous and nonpartisan Venezuelan students hit the streets in 2007, their logo—a stencil of a clenched white fist—was *exactly* the same as that used by Otpor, and appears in AEI literature.

Those students at the forefront of 2007 protests nevertheless insisted that their movement was spontaneous and that they had nothing to do with the Venezuelan opposition or existing political parties. The connection was obvious even at the time, however, and was confirmed afterward when almost *every* student leader quickly joined opposition political parties. The most visible at the time, Yon Goicoechea, was later awarded a prize from the Cato Institute named for the

12   Carlos Chirinos, "Capturan 'paramilitares' en Venezuela," BBC Mundo, May 9, 2004, news.bbc.co.uk.
13   Stratfor, "Venezuela: The Marigold Revolution?" October 5, 2007, stratfor.com.

founder of neoliberalism, Milton Friedman—a fitting achievement. When the third act resumed in early 2014, these same claims of nonviolence, spontaneity, and independence from discredited opposition parties were again on full display.

When I challenged AEI about its support for an undeniably violent Venezuelan opposition, Gene Sharp offered the best proof that apparently principled advocates of nonviolence can naively serve the powerful just as easily as they serve the powerless, writing in an email:

> If we had refused the request for a workshop for the Venezuelan resisters, some of them would possibly have concluded the "only" option to be another coup d'état, riots, assassinations, or even a foreign invasion, as in Iraq ... Would you have recommended that the dissident Venezuelans instead use violence?[14]

The face of this new right-wing fringe is undoubtedly Lorent Saleh, a fiery former leader of the Venezuelan youth group United Active Youth of Venezuela (JAVU). Like its predecessors, JAVU has gathered funds from a variety of US government sources, which allowed it to gain notoriety quickly as the hardline wing of opposition street movements. After he was expelled from JAVU, Saleh went on to join Operation Freedom, a clandestine network founded in 2011 with the support of Miami-based Swede Ulf Erlingsson.

---

14   George Ciccariello-Maher and Eva Golinger, "Making Excuses for Empire: A Reply to the Self-Appointed Defenders of the AEI," *MRZine*, August 8, 2008. Note the language of "resisters" and "dissidents."

A strange bird indeed, Erlingsson was a conscientious objector in Sweden and is a self-professed antiwar activist today, who somehow manages to square his support for Dennis Kucinich's presidential campaign with his support for the bloody and unconstitutional Honduran coup of 2009. Despite an official adherence to nonviolence, moreover, the stated aim of Erlingsson's organization is "to overthrow the Castro-communist dictatorship in Venezuela." The organization's primary spokesperson abroad is Cuban-Venezuelan actress María Conchita Alonso, sister of the paramilitary-training Robert. Alonso provoked controversy when she celebrated Chávez's death during a television interview, adding that "it would have been better for him to die slowly of his illness in jail." (She made headlines a year later after appearing in an ad supporting the racist, anti-immigrant Tea Party candidate for California governor, Tim Donnelly.) To top it all off, one of the few public members of this clandestine "nonviolent" network is none other than Ángel Vivas.

The best proof of Operation Freedom's selective embrace of nonviolence is Saleh himself, who currently presides over the organization from a prison cell in Caracas. As a member of Operation Freedom, Saleh is alleged to have traveled to Costa Rica, where he met with organizers of the 2002 coup and a veritable demon from Venezuela's past: Henry López Sisco. The former head of the Venezuelan intelligence services, López Sisco was tied to almost every massacre of the 1980s, including the Caracazo. To this day, he is on close terms with Cuban-Venezuelan anticommunist terrorist mastermind Luis Posada Carriles, a former CIA operative convicted of bombing a Cuban airliner in 1976, killing seventy-three people. In 2011, Venezuela requested López Sisco's extradition for his role in the 1986 massacre of nine young organizers in Yumare, but Costa Rica refused.

It is ironic, to say the least, that someone claiming to oppose a repressive government would consort with the central architect of Venezuelan state terrorism. But it was in Colombia that Saleh's objectives truly became clear. There he participated in activities organized by the fascist National Alliance for Freedom and alongside the openly neo-Nazi Third Force organization, during which he admitted that the Venezuelan opposition was planning a coup. Later, Saleh apparently infiltrated a Colombian military base, where he acquired training, and this self-described defender of human rights even met personally with the most egregious abuser of the human rights of Colombians, Álvaro Uribe.

Saleh's big mouth would be his undoing, however. In a series of Skype videos that have since gone public, Saleh boasted about plans to purchase sniper rifles, hire explosives experts and "anticommunist" mercenaries, blow up bridges and nightclubs, and send ten well-armed and "indoctrinated" troops to Caracas and five to Valencia to carry out a "cleansing" of Chavistas. In the videos, Saleh bragged about his relations with Uribe. When the Colombian government of Juan Manuel Santos finally deported Saleh, Uribe—who now enjoys immunity from prosecution as a senator—was the first to denounce the move on Twitter as a sign of complicity with the Venezuelan government.

Lorent Saleh is certainly on the far right-wing fringe of a Venezuelan opposition that at least occasionally tries to maintain a distance from violent extremists. But what is revealing is that this same opposition today dignifies this figure—a fascist sympathizer, avowed terrorist, and proponent of social "cleansing"—with the label "political prisoner." After winning the National Assembly elections of December 2015, the first major piece of legislation that the opposition drafted and approved was a controversial amnesty law that, had it not been quickly struck down by the Supreme Court, could have seen Saleh and others walk free.

4

MILITIAS AND REVOLUTIONARY COLLECTIVES

In October 2014, violence was in the air and on the tip of every tongue, and not only due to the opposition protests. On the first day of the month, the young Chavista firebrand Robert Serra was brutally murdered alongside his partner. Serra had been tied up in his apartment and stabbed more than thirty times, and the Maduro government placed the blame squarely on Colombian paramilitaries. While circumstances remain unclear, Serra himself had recently denounced Lorent Saleh's ties to that king-pin of Colombian reaction, Álvaro Uribe. Despite Venezuela's sharp polarization and violent street crime, political murders of this kind had been almost unheard of.

Scarcely a week later, on October 7, one of the most mysterious events of recent Venezuelan history ensued. In the rundown Quinta Crespo neighborhood, near Caracas' old city center, the specialized police forces of the CICPC clashed with a little-known Chavista group, the March 5th Revolutionary Collective, in broad daylight, leading to an hours-long standoff. During a lull in the fighting, the group's leader, José Odreman, spoke to the press, insisting that if anything happened to him, the guilt would fall directly on interior minister Miguel Rodríguez Torres. When asked if there was any connection between the police siege and Serra's murder, Odreman—himself a former police officer—replied cryptically, "Math doesn't lie."

When the smoke cleared hours later, there were five dead, Odreman included, in what according to some accounts looked more like an execution than anything else. According to the police, those killed were members of a criminal gang guilty of extortion and even murder. Just three weeks before the clash, the right-wing newspaper *El Nacional* had published a critical exposé of Odreman and his collective's operations in the Cotiza neighborhood to the north, recognizing their positive role in the community while also accusing them of intimidating neighbors and demanding protection payments.[1]

But revolutionary collectives like the March 5th have long been the Bolivarian Revolution's most ferocious defenders, and while it's certainly possible for an armed revolutionary group to embrace criminal activity, many Chavistas would hesitate to take the word of the media or the state over that of the grassroots. To make things even more complex, a photo showing Odreman and Serra together began to circulate, stoking controversy and conspiracy theories. For those more sympathetic to the collectives, this was—in the words of

---

1 Angélica Lugo, "Cotiza es centro de operaciones de 100 colectivos de Caracas," *El Nacional*, September 14, 2014, el-nacional.com.

longtime   militant   Roland   Denis—Chavismo's   "first
massacre."

The term "collectives" is sharply debated in Venezuela today.
On a most basic level, it refers to a broad range of grassroots
groups organized in different ways and toward different ends.
Whenever a small group of neighbors, grassroots organizers,
or activists come together under the aegis of the Bolivarian
Revolution, we could say that a collective has been born. But
most Venezuelans—Chavistas and anti-Chavistas alike—tend
to use the term in a more specific way: to refer to the armed
self-defense militias that emerged in poor barrios nationwide
during the 1980s and 1990s, prior to the Bolivarian Revolution.

These militias were organic outgrowths of conditions in
the barrios themselves. They emerged when neighbors got
together and armed themselves to stamp out the drug trade
and make their neighborhoods safe from gang violence and
police repression. Since the police themselves were often
complicit in the drug trade and the violence it wrought, the
earliest collectives drove out the *narcos* and the police in the
same gesture, taking responsibility for security in their local
neighborhoods (some areas have not allowed the police to
enter for more than twenty-five years). Unlike militias in
many other parts of the world, these groups tended to be
politically conscious: committed to communism and hostile
to the bureaucratic central state.

As a result, many collectives supported Chávez's coup in
1992, mobilized the grassroots for his election in 1998, and
took up arms during the 2002 coup—not to attack the

constitutional order, but to protect and restore it by playing a key role in reversing the coup and returning Chávez to power. Without these groups, and the support of the radical grassroots more generally, the Bolivarian Revolution most likely would not have survived past 2002. The fact that the government depended so heavily on armed revolutionary movements ultimately helped to radicalize the process as a whole. The collectives, the bedrock of the Revolution, have consistently attacked corruption, defended their local autonomy, and pressured those in power to move more quickly toward socialism.

As a historic counterweight to the centralized state, the collectives often clashed with Chávez himself, blockading their neighborhoods with burning barricades and prominently displaying weapons as a demonstration of revolutionary autonomy. But never before had the government drawn blood as it did in Quinta Crespo. The revolutionary collectives so central to the Bolivarian Revolution had been born under very different circumstances, however, winning their autonomy from a hostile state by force and at great cost. While this was no vaccine against corruption—some who fought the drug trade quickly turned to embrace it—today's collectives are a much more mixed bag.

Some maintain a close relationship with the state and have benefited significantly from access to government funds. Others have opted for political and financial autonomy, taking a more radical line against the state as an institution that they see—even in the hands of Chavismo—to be corrupt and corrupting. Still others—and here things get murkier--have used their authority and even their weapons to seize territory and manage underground commerce for their own private ends. If this picture is not complex enough, many collectives also count police and ex-police among their ranks, including some purged from police forces for corruption and violence. The line between the state and the grassroots has become dangerously blurred indeed.

After Quinta Crespo, a painful debate ensued within the ranks of radical Chavismo: were those killed by the police revolutionary heroes or common criminals? Firsthand testimony emerged to support both possibilities, but a surprising number of revolutionaries swallowed the official position hook, line, and sinker, uncritically echoing government declarations that the March 5th was not a "real" collective, was not truly revolutionary, and was simply using the name "collective" as a cover for criminal activity. Many appear to have forgotten that the police are just as likely to be involved in violent crime as any collective—if not much more so.[2] At any rate, the line between the two in contemporary Venezuela is less and less clear, a fact only underlined by Odreman's own history as a police officer.

For their part, the Venezuelan opposition and its wealthy constituents are deathly afraid of the collectives, a term that has come to embody everything they fear about Chavismo itself: dark skin and red shirts materializing without

---

2   Official data from 2009 indicates that up to 20 percent of all crimes are committed by the police themselves. "20% de los delitos son cometidos por uniformados," *Últimas Noticias*, March 19, 2012, ultimasnoticias.com.

warning on a phalanx of motorcycles. Circulating like torturous phantoms in the opposition imaginary, these only vaguely identifiable groups have been deemed guilty of imagined massacres. During the opposition protests of 2014, the panic and paranoia reached shrill new heights. One of the most widely shared posts on the opposition blog *Caracas Chronicles*, for example, included videos claiming to show armed collectives firing on opposition protesters with live rounds—only later did it become clear that those in the video were actually police firing tear gas and rubber bullets.[3]

For the former commune minister Reinaldo Iturriza, this fear of the collectives is no mistake but points directly toward their true significance: "The collectives are synonymous with organization, not violence." It is the organized poor that the rich fear most.[4]

A month after the killings, security was tight at the March 5th Socialist City in Cotiza, the operational base of those killed in Quinta Crespo. The impressiveness of this compound, a sort of hilltop fortress due north of downtown Caracas, where city streets climb abruptly and dead-end into El Ávila National Park, already suggests that the March 5th was much more than the "criminal gang" the police

3   The post, which also falsely claims to show a murder by police, was later altered but not retracted. Audrey Dacosta, "19F—The Night Venezuela Finally Imploded," *Caracas Chronicles*, February 19, 2014, caracaschronicles. com.

4   Reinaldo Iturriza, "Los colectivos son sinónimo de organización, no de violecia," *Ciudad CCS*, March 10, 2014, ciudadccs.info.

have argued. The guard post at the foot of the hill bears a photo of Odreman; the walls are adorned with images of Odreman and other revolutionary "martyrs." These include a large mural of "Juancho" Montoya and Eliécer Otaiza, two revolutionaries killed under similarly suspicious circumstances. The first died during the opposition protests in February 2014, apparently from friendly cross-fire, and the second—like Robert Serra—was tortured and killed only two months later. All told, 2014 was a bloody year for Chavismo.

Representatives of more than a hundred revolutionary collectives had gathered at the Socialist City for a secret meeting called in response to the events of Quinta Crespo. One of the main organizers of the meeting was Roland Denis, one of the sharpest left-wing critics of Chavismo. Despite his critical tone—for which he is often touted by anarchists and anti-Chavistas abroad—Denis is still very much a Chavista. When Chávez died, Denis penned a heartfelt eulogy to the "passionate irreverence" and rebellious spirit of the late leader. Since Chávez's death, however, Denis's tone has grown more intransigent in some widely read articles—one of which asks rhetorically, "Who's Ready to Tell Maduro to Go to Hell?"—bordering on what many Chavistas would consider heresy.[5]

The police massacre in Quinta Crespo represented, for Denis, an attack on the "pure nobility" of the Venezuelan

---

5   Roland Denis, "Chavez and Sabino Show the Way," *Venezuela Analysis*, March 9, 2013; "¿Quién está dispuesto?," *Aporrea.org*, April 17, 2014.

people, who in all their complexity and vices embody the beauty of a real, concrete revolution. Collective members may not be highly educated, he told me, but "they are Chavistas, period," and despite their ideological limitations, "the collectives have a class dignity and a pride in defending what's theirs. That's where the revolution is reborn, by the craziest routes." While his view is certainly romantic, Denis finds it much more naive to simply take the word of the police and the state, as some collectives did. Some, like the Alexis Vive Collective, met with interior minister Rodríguez Torres—and in so doing, Denis argues, committed a form of class treason. At that point, for Denis, "you're my enemy," because "you've co-signed my death."[6]

Like Denis, the collectives gathered in Cotiza did not consider themselves enemies of the Bolivarian Revolution but its most ferocious defenders. They came together not to oppose the government, but to discuss and approve a document that would be sent to Maduro himself proposing a direct dialogue between the collectives and the government, with the goal of radicalizing the Revolution as a whole.[7] In it, they echoed

------

6 Needless to say, members of the Alexis Vive Collective, the driving force behind the El Panal Commune that I discuss in Chapter 6, would reject this assessment. In an open letter to Denis, they denounced what they call "pseudo-collectives" that engage in criminal activity and thereby "disgrace the true revolutionary praxis of the collectives." Colectivo y Fundación Alexis Vive, "Carta abierta a Roland Denis y a quienes pretenden enlodar la historia del barrio, del Colectivo, de la Comuna," November 1, 2014, aporrea.org.

7 "Documento-Acuerdo entre los Colectivos de Trabajo Revolucionario—Movimiento de Defensa Popular Juan Montoya y el Gobierno Nacional," November 2014, aporrea.org.

Chávez's oft-repeated insistence that the Bolivarian Revolution is "peaceful, but not unarmed," arguing that the collectives themselves constitute a form of "street democracy" that emerged in response to the "genocide" of the Caracazo.

The meeting was heated, somewhere between respectful discussion and a defiant political rally. There was a consensus in the room that for the collectives to lay down their weapons was simply not an option in a society in which the state itself cannot provide basic security for the poor, and many doubted the motivations of those government officials who would prefer the grassroots to be unarmed. If the government was at all serious about disarming criminals, one speaker interjected, then the first step would be to "disarm all the police, and don't leave a single *paco* with a single bullet." Until this happened, the collectives themselves would not give up a single bullet or they would be left defenseless in the face of organized crime, the right wing, and the state. Thunderous chants of "*¡Ni una bala!* Not a single bullet!" echoed across the hall.

Despite refusing to disarm individually, the collectives nevertheless recognized that "the arms of the people"—military-grade weaponry—should remain in the barracks with the official armed forces and Bolivarian militias. They also recognized the need to purge their own ranks, disarming and expelling those using the name "collective" to engage in corruption or violence. Toward this end, the document they drafted proposed regular meetings with government officials in order to maintain—not disrupt—the historically symbiotic relationship between grassroots movements and the state, even offering their services to help fight the "economic war" against smuggling and speculation. "We collectives are the spearhead" of the revolution, one speaker proclaimed.

The turning point in public debates about the Quinta Crespo killings came when former vice president José Vicente Rangel weighed in on the subject. Rangel, who rose to prominence denouncing human rights abuses, torture, and massacre under the old regime, enjoys an unparalleled level of respect on the subject of state violence and can speak more openly than most. So when he published a blistering editorial in Venezuela's most widely read newspaper entitled "Operation Massacre," the impact was instantaneous.[8] "Nothing is more dangerous for a society," Rangel wrote, "than what occurs when the demons within police institutions—inspired by sordid conceptions of public order and state security— escape. That is, when governments lose control of them and they begin to engage in politics of their own." The police, Rangel suggested, will inevitably step in to fill any vacuum left by the state, pointing to ten recent cases of extrajudicial killings carried out by police forces. "The way that CICPC commandos killed five Chavista militants" instead of detaining them "is unacceptable in a democracy."

Only days after Rangel's op-ed, Otro Beta organizers in Petare told me similar stories of extrajudicial killings by the police. They explained how former drug dealers and gang members from the barrio who had turned toward political

8   José Vicente Rangel, "Operación massacre," *Últimas Noticias*, October 20, 2014, aporrea.org.

organizing were nevertheless targeted by corrupt and violent police, citing several execution-style murders. One case, the killing of Manuel "Manolo" Mosquera in July 2014, stands out in particular. After many years of criminal activity, Mosquera had reinvented himself as a local activist, encouraging at-risk youth to follow a different path. Not long after Mosquera met with President Maduro, who praised his efforts at turning his life around, Mosquera was executed by the CICPC in what Otro Beta organizers compare to a Colombian-style "cleansing" operation.

There is an entire segment of the Venezuelan government, they explained, that sees *mano dura*, or hardline policing, as the only solution to violent crime, especially when the population demands that something, anything, be done. They explained how this approach, which they denounce as "fascist," was best represented by Rodríguez Torres, then interior minister, whom Odreman had preemptively blamed for his own foretold death. But just as the Otro Beta organizers were explaining this to me, a radio program playing in the background announced that Maduro had just sacked Rodríguez Torres as a result of the political fallout of the Quinta Crespo massacre. This victory, however small, showed that Maduro—like Chávez before him—could be pushed to the left by popular power from below. However, later policing strategies, like the heavy-handed "Operation Free the People," launched in 2015, show that the hardline approaches Rodríguez Torres had championed was not gone for good.

~

The underlying tension between a revolutionary movement that has taken power and its most militant grassroots supporters remains unresolved. The questions posed most sharply by the collectives have continued to bubble up incessantly in debates that have swirled about revolutionary unity and discipline ever since Chávez, the embodiment of both, died. If Chávez was uniquely able to walk a fine line between grassroots movements and state institutions, the years since his death have seen old conflicts re-emerge with a vengeance.

Nearly victorious in the 2013 election, the opposition swarmed at the sight of fresh blood. In response to mounting political and economic instability, the besieged Maduro government has shown a tendency toward closing ranks and hushing more radical voices, even openly attacking the irresponsibility of the "ultra-left." But this has only provoked even looser tongues and sparked an open debate over the role of the radical left within revolutionary movements. The ultra-left in Venezuela often refers broadly to a handful of critical intellectuals—from the anarchistic Roland Denis himself to those like political scientist Nicmer Evans and others grouped around the Trotskyist Marea Socialista (Socialist Tide) current, and even the website Aporrea.org, a sort of clearinghouse for all things revolutionary.

Unsurprisingly, the question of who could claim a monopoly on revolutionary discourse first emerged in debates about the state's monopoly of armed violence. One of the first hints that a clash was brewing beneath the surface came in response to the government's Disarmament Law. Proposed in 2013, the law sought to respond to one of the revolution's most pressing challenges—violent crime—by getting guns off the street; it gained the support of many grassroots activists in the process. Many radical Chavistas, however, pointed to the historic role of armed struggle and armed self-defense, wondering out loud if the Chávez government would have survived the 2002 coup were it not for armed civilians organized into collectives.

Critics were openly skeptical of a law that seemed more geared toward assuaging middle-class fears than truly confronting the drug cartels behind the violence—after all, the real criminals would not hand over their weapons so easily. This concern seemed validated when the first public display of decommissioned weapons occurred, of all places, in the revolutionary neighborhood of 23 de Enero, a hotbed of armed revolutionary collectives, not gang activity. Speaking on live television in August 2013 next to a table covered with all types of firearms, Maduro praised the collectives for handing over nearly a hundred weapons, destined for destruction. But these old rifles and sawed-off shotguns were not the best weapons the collectives possessed—for whom was this performance staged?

When the Chavista television personality Alberto Nolia used his evening program on state channel VTV to openly attack the law as ineffective and replete with "petit-bourgeois" prejudices—even scrolling the hashtag #ChávezWanted ThePeopleArmed across the bottom of the screen—his show was quickly yanked off the air. Nolia was only one of several critics who soon clashed with the Bolivarian leadership. That same month, Nicmer Evans lost his program on the national radio network, joining others like the leftist professor Heiber Barreto, the ex-guerrilla Toby Valderrama, and the radical Marxist historian Vladimir Acosta, all of whom were effectively pushed off the air earlier in the year through a variety of tactics, from scheduling changes to outright dismissals.

These were followed the next year by Vanessa Davies, a former high-ranking PSUV member who lost her evening television program, *Contragolpe* (Counterattack), and has since been pushed out of party leadership. Most shocking of all was the departure of Mario Silva's combative *La Hojilla* (The Razor), a must-watch among everyday Chavistas. Loathed by the opposition, Silva made a name for himself by mocking and denouncing anti-Chavistas in the most insulting ways possible. *La Hojilla* was suddenly yanked off the air a week after the opposition released a mysterious secret recording in which Silva appears to denounce corruption among some high-ranking Chavista leaders.[9] (To the delight of many, Silva's program recently returned to the screen, repeating a pattern that held under Chávez, in which hardline voices that rock the boat are temporarily ostracized before later being welcomed back into the fold.)

The opposition media gladly and cynically took up the cause of those on the radical left they had never agreed with before, deeming them victims of "censorship" plain and simple. But at stake in this debate is more than just criticism versus discipline, hushing radical voices in favor of a

---

9 "Esta es la transcripción completa del audio presentado por Ismael García," *Noticias 24*, May 20, 2013, noticias24.com.

smoothly unified front. It is also a debate between militants about what constitutes a truly revolutionary outlook. After all, the critics have been undeniably more openly combative toward Maduro than they were toward Chávez, highlighting what they see as the president's willingness to negotiate and compromise with the enemies of the revolution. But Chávez also did so often and strategically, and himself attacked radicals on many occasions, even going so far as to wrongly blame the Chilean ultra-left for having undermined the Allende government prior to the Pinochet coup.

Against some of the most vocal critics of Maduro's policies, other revolutionaries with even deeper roots in concrete organizing have responded by insisting that critique without action is merely empty posturing. Revolutions are difficult and messy affairs, they argue, and it is unrealistic to expect that they will remain pure in the face of a protracted and complicated struggle against unwavering enemies. One memorable piece of satire by on-the-ground revolutionary militants from the barrios jokingly suggested that if only Roland Denis were named president and Nicmer Evans his vice president, the Revolution would finally have achieved the level of purity and perfection that they promise.

C.L.R. James once wrote that "the cruelties of property and privilege are always more ferocious than the revenges of poverty and oppression."[10] If we had any reason to doubt this

---

10   C.L.R. James, *The Black Jacobins: Toussaint L'Ouverture and the San Domingo Revolution* (New York: Vintage, 1989 [1963]), 88–89.

observation—that the brutality of elites tends to exceed that of the poor—-we need only look at the opposition protests of 2014 and the new right-wing youth who led them. We could even extend this observation further, to highlight the even more brutal desperation to return to the old status quo, to restore the feudal privileges of deposed Venezuelan elites. Here, the best evidence is the brief coup against Chávez in 2002, which saw more protesters killed by police in a matter of hours than in previous years, and during which Chavistas were hunted and beaten by braying mobs not of the poor and dark-skinned but of the wealthy and white.

Drawing upon the simultaneous revolutions in France and Haiti, James distinguished between the Jacobins and the sansculottes—the radical leadership and the grassroots base. "The Jacobins," he argued, "were authoritarian . . . they wished to act with the people and for them," whereas the sansculottes "were extreme democrats: they wanted the direct government of the people by the people; if they demanded a dictatorship against the aristocrats they wished to exercise it themselves."[11] The revolutionary violence of the poor is not brutality for brutality's sake but instead a strange paradox: radically egalitarian brutality in favor of a directly democratic dictatorship of the oppressed. Despite what the Venezuelan opposition claims, the Chavista government has not unleashed this kind of popular brutality but has contained it. What would happen if the Chavistas no longer held back the legitimate ferocity of the poor?

---

11   Ibid., 276.

Hugo Chávez, a Jacobin by James's definition, often acted *with* the people rather than *for* them, but his personality and proximity to power inevitably kept him at arm's length from the grassroots. The revolution was never his to begin with: it preceded him, exceeded him, and today outlives him— because, like the sansculottes, Venezuelan revolutionaries are dedicated to the slow and difficult construction of radically democratic and participatory socialist alternatives. This promise, however, is also a warning that Nicolás Maduro neglects at his own peril: it is not the Venezuelan Jacobins that will save the Bolivarian Revolution, but the sansculottes.

5
THE COMMUNE IN PROGRESS

In Venezuela, nothing is more communal than *sancocho*. The process of making a *sancocho*, a sort of mixed stew often cooked over an open fire in a massive pot, is far more important than its precise ingredients. This weekend tradition might see one neighbor provide the chicken or beef; another pluck a few plantains or their stout cousins, *topochos*, off their bush; and still others contribute yucca or a variety of other, untranslatable local tubers: *malanga, ocumo, ñame*.

This tradition reflects a collective ethic still deeply rooted in the Venezuelan countryside—so much so that the word *sancocho* is often interchangeable with a party or celebration. The culture of the collective stew extends to the cities as well, or at least to the barrios that surround them: if you stroll through the wealthy Altamira district of Caracas on a Sunday, you may see well-heeled Venezuelans drinking espressos outside Italian bakeries, but climb into the barrios and you will see smoke billowing from open flames and neighbors coming together to celebrate togetherness itself. So it's no surprise that many a commune has been born around a *sancocho* pot. For many, in fact, coming together to discuss something as important as community self-management without sharing a meal would be unthinkable.

This is certainly the case for the El Maizal Commune. When the commune was born in early 2009, Ángel Prado was there at the steaming pot, which in this corn-producing region would certainly have contained plenty of those rings of corn sliced right through the cob that are still called by their indigenous name, *jojoto*. Prado himself had been a security guard until just the day before, but he has long since swapped his uniform for a T-shirt, muddy boots, and the calloused hands of a farmer. Back in March 2009, he and others—upon hearing that Chávez was on his way to visit their small town—walked off the job to await his arrival. "We came alongside the commotion of the people, we made a stew, set up a tent, and discussed. We called an assembly and we waited for Chávez."

The name of El Maizal Commune tells much of the story: it means "the cornfield." When I spoke with Prado—an elected spokesperson for the commune—he was standing in the middle of almost 2,000 acres of growing corn, more than three square miles of autonomous and communally self-managed production. To foreign eyes, El Maizal corn might look over-dried, nearly dead, but this is only because it's not meant for eating fresh. Corn here is destined for grinding, providing the fine flour for Venezuela's staple *arepas*. El Maizal straddles the border of the states of Lara and Portuguesa in Venezuela's southwestern heartland (Portuguesa is known as Venezuela's "granary" for its agricultural production).

Massive *samán* trees dot the landscape, anchoring history in space under their wide canopies. Venerated by indigenous communities, these trees are said to have gained their name when an Arawak shaman was killed under one. Simón Bolívar himself sought shelter under nearby *samánes* during the 1813 Battle of Araure, and once visited the most famous example of the species—the legendary Samán de Güere—which is said to have lived more than a thousand years and which boasted a sprawling 576-foot canopy before recently being felled by lightning strikes. It was there, in 1982, that, amid the crisis of the corrupt two-party system, a young Hugo Chávez swore an oath to overthrow an increasingly corrupt and violent two-party democracy. Almost exactly a decade later, the Bolivarian Revolutionary Movement would make good on his promise by launching a failed coup in February of 1992.

This area boasts a long history of struggle on and for the land itself. It was here, on these lands, that the elite political system pioneered its land policies and that local peasants fought back. Before the arrival of democracy in 1958, this territory was populated by both small individual plots of land but also collective plots and even communal ownership, where neighbors shared and cultivated common land. While the 1961 Land Reform promised to help poor farmers by distributing the land, in reality the effect was the opposite. Instead of breaking up large landholdings and distributing these lands to the poor, the new democratic government kicked *campesinos* off public lands—destroying pre-existing communal forms—handed the most productive terrain over to business interests loyal to the ruling Democratic Action (AD) party.

Prado calls the Land Reform a "farce," and he's right: when all was said and done, most of the land distributed had been public rather than private. A third of those supposedly benefiting from the land reform dropped out due to a lack of support, and 90 percent never gained ownership rights.[1] The lands that today constitute the commune were no exception: they passed into private hands and local farmers were forced out, with only a handful being hired back as wage laborers. Many others fled to the cities, populating the urban barrios. Those who stayed were pushed off the fertile valley floor and uphill into the mountains, some intermingling with the armed guerrillas who had made their homes there voluntarily to fight what they considered a repressive and undemocratic regime.

When Chávez was elected, Prado and many others had a natural affinity for this poor kid from the countryside who had become president. He looked like them, talked like them, and danced and sang the *joropo* ballads of the Venezuelan flatlands that they knew. But the affinity ran deeper. The first task of the Chávez government was to rewrite the Constitution in a collective and participatory way, with popular neighborhood assemblies formed to discuss, debate, make proposals, and ultimately approve the 1999 Constitution. According to Prado, it

---

1   Gregory Wilpert, "Land for People Not for Profit in Venezuela," in P. Rosset, R. Patel, and M. Courville, eds., *Promised Land: Competing Visions of Agrarian Reform* (New York: Food First, 2006), 251. See also Ciccariello-Maher, *We Created Chávez*, 206–7.

was through this process that "the people began to understand that laws are not eternal and that we can modify them."

The participatory nature of the constitutional process reflected the radical content of the Constitution. The country's new Magna Carta rejected the large rural landholdings known as *latifundios*, where land often lay idle while nearby residents went hungry. The Constitution declared these "contrary to the interests of society" and recognized the validity of other competing forms of property: associative, cooperative, and "collective ownership." In 2001, the Constitution was followed by a radical Land Law that set into motion the kind of redistribution promised but never delivered in 1961. Ten years later, more than 10 million acres of land had been distributed to small farmers, half from public lands and half from land expropriated by the government after being deemed idle. More than a million Venezuelans— over half the rural population—benefited.[2]

Even then, however, with land being seized and redistributed nationwide, Prado confesses that few locals expected El Maizal would be also be expropriated from its private owner. "It never crossed our minds that this plantation could be touched . . . It was almost like a religious question." When Chávez's helicopter finally touched down, it kicked up a cloud of dust in the valley and appared to bow the corn stalks into secular prayer. then "the seemingly impossible happened": The president unexpectedly declared that since

2   Gregory Wilpert, "Chávez's Legacy of Land Reform for Venezuela," *Review of Agrarian Studies* 3(2) (2014), ras.org.

the land was unproductive, it would be expropriated and handed over to the people. In Prado's words, "The commune was born March 5, 2009," four years to the day before Chávez's death. While the birth of El Maizal might therefore seem like a classic populist narrative of a great leader bringing salvation from above, the organizers who would come to form the commune had already gathered around the *sancocho* before he arrived, and their fight was far from over.

Chávez declared that the expropriated lands would be self-managed by the local farmers in conjunction with the state. But as soon as his helicopter took off, Prado explains, "These lands had a new owner." While the government had seized the lands from the private owners, they did not hand them over directly to the newborn commune but instead placed the land in the custody of the state-run agricultural corporation, Corporación Venezolana de Alimentos (CVAL), which oversees and coordinates food production and distribution nationwide. "The gates stayed shut," Prado insists, describing how, rather than producing, corrupt state employees were instead "stealing and dismantling everything."

There is little reason to doubt Prado's account. Corruption has been rife in CVAL and in Venezuela's food production and distribution network as a whole. In 2015, the nearby Negro Miguel Commune seized land from CVAL under similar circumstances after documenting on video the lack of cultivation.[3] In early 2016, a national police operation named

---

3   "Corredor Territorial Negro Miguel Toman Tierras de CVAL," Alba TV, January 9, 2015, albatv.org.

Attack the Weevil targeted high-level corruption in the food sector, leading to dozens of arrests and the confiscation of more than twenty tons of price-controlled food. The president of CVAL was arrested, along with his administrative assistant and her mother—who was president of the state-run Bicentenario supermarket chain. Investigators claim that the three conspired to embezzle price-controlled food, selling it at exorbitant black-market rates to private restaurants and supermarkets.

In El Maizal, local farmers were ecstatic when Chávez expropriated the land, but quickly disappointed to find that CVAL had no intention of hiring them, except as menial wage laborers—hardly different from when the land was in private hands. Communal organizers continued to hold popular assemblies in nearby communities, incorporating more communal councils into their growing commune and involving larger sectors of the neighboring population in their decision-making process. Politically strengthened by this support and participation of the local community, the El Maizal Commune again demanded access to the land and were finally granted a small 370-acre plot of marginal, unproductive land. Undeterred, the *comuneros* planted black beans and continued to organize neighboring communities to join the commune.

Even on this tiny plot of land, they were far more productive than both the previous private landholder and the state corporation with all its resources. Their combined agricultural and political success—a strong black bean harvest and increasing support in nearby communities—led Chávez to return later in 2009 to broadcast his television program, *Aló*

Presidente. With the cornfield and a sprawling *samán* tree as his backdrop, the president confirmed that the lands should belong to the commune itself, not to the state. But once again, Chávez climbed back into his helicopter and left, and, much to the chagrin of the commune and to Chávez himself, the orders were never fully carried out. Prado claims that the president called to reprimand local political leaders for dragging their feet, but opposition to the commune within the local state institutions was strong.

Frustrated organizers decided to take matters into their own hands: in early 2010 they occupied the land and called an assembly with state administrators, refusing to leave unless CVAL agreed to split the land with them fifty-fifty. Prado believes that the state company, in complicity with the old private landowners, was simply waiting for the commune to collapse so things could get back to normal. While this may or may not have been true, the state and the private sector both agreed on one thing: "They were betting that the poor were born to be poor, that the poor can't be administrators," according to Prado. But they were wrong, and finally in 2014, these *comuneros* used the leverage provided by Chávez's "Golpe de Timón" speech to throw out the state company and take over the land themselves.

Today, the El Maizal Commune manages this entire massive cornfield, directly contradicting such condescending assumptions about the poor. Production is managed under the aegis of a direct and communal EPS—the most radical form of Venezuela's socialist enterprises. This means that the communal parliament—composed of delegates of all the communal councils and socialist enterprises—makes all decisions about the production process, and the entire surplus is reinvested in the community itself. In 2014, El Maizal harvested 1,000 acres of corn—generating a surplus of more than $1 million—along with raising 400 animals and a variety of fruits and beans, even coffee. And 2015 marked their first year harvesting all of the land, more than 2,000 acres in total: the commune produced 2.5 million kilos of corn, 30,000 kilos of coffee, and more than 50,000 liters of milk, alongside other products.[4]

State officials have confirmed El Maizal's claims to efficient communal production, recognizing that the commune's productivity per acre is "twice the national average."[5] All of this makes El Maizal, without a doubt, one of the largest, most productive, and most politically successful communes in all of Venezuela. For some critics the communes are a fundamentally populist project, by which they mean they are created by state leaders and depend on the goodwill of the state. Others, similarly skeptical, would argue that to begin from the perspective of a commune as productive as El Maizal is to cherry-pick a success story. In fact, neither view is accurate, since El Maizal was born neither from above nor easily,

---

4　"Más de 2 millones de maíz industrializará este año comuna El Maizal," *La Prensa*, September 6, 2015, laprensalara.com.

5　An interview with the economist Juan Bautista Arias, "Otro modo de producir es possible," *Ciudad CCS*, February 18, 2015, ciudadccs.info. An official for Lara State confirmed that levels of production exceeded both regular levels for the area and national averages. "Jonás Reyes verifica la producción de El Maizal," *La Prensa*, October 1, 2014, laprensalara.com.

but instead from a constant and unrelenting struggle to carve out a communal space against the steepest odds and even against the state.

The commune does indeed manage significant state resources, helping to decide how funding from the central state is distributed to build public housing—managing the construction of 500 homes through Misión Vivienda—and to provide health care and education for the local community. These are important elements of a broader communal project that aspires "to transform those communities, to beautify them, to build roads, to consolidate the educational and health infrastructure," in Prado's words. Beyond channeling these funds and taking advantage of low-interest loans, however, El Maizal receives almost no state funds. Rather than depending on the state, it depends on its own productivity.

Furthermore, despite the leverage provided by Chávez, El Maizal's relationship with government institutions has been one of direct and frontal combat, from its clashes with the state agricultural company to the antagonism of local elected officials. According to Prado—echoing a refrain shared by almost every commune I have visited—the commune's "principal enemies" are actually Chavistas: local mayors and state governors feel threatened by successful experiments that cut into their resources and make them look bad. Even the local Socialist Party (PSUV) behaves as though its "task is to destroy the commune, to finish the commune, to denounce, disparage, demoralize, divide, and extinguish the commune, to disperse the people," Prado contends. "We *comuneros* share very little with the governing party."

Even local sustainability—the primary goal of the communes—seems to threaten the economic status quo. In the current context of economic shortages, few products are harder to find than the most universally popular brand of corn flour, Harina Pan, which is produced by the private conglomerate Polar. El Maizal's goal is to cut out private corporations like Polar by "bringing a finished product to the community." By providing a diverse range of basic goods—from flour for *arepas* to the beans, cheese, and chicken that go inside of them—the community will become increasingly self-sufficient, with the commune at its heart. Today, however, most of El Maizal's raw corn is destined for state and private mills, and several commune activists expressed frustration that the government has not been more supportive of their attempts to move up the productive chain and mill their own corn flour.

Here as elsewhere, this three-way clash between the state, the private sector, and the communes can have fatal consequences. In 2013, as Prado and other activists were driving to a community assembly, two men on motorcycles sprayed Prado's truck with gunfire before fleeing.[6] While it is unclear who precisely orchestrated the attack, it comes as little surprise in a country that has seen more than 300 *campesino* organizers murdered with impunity in the past fifteen years. While the assumption is that large landholders are usually to blame, the killings are often contracted out to hired guns known as

---

6   Ernesto Cazal, "De entre las espigas nace la esperanza," *Ciudad CCS*, January 25, 2014, ciudadccs.info.

sicarios, making it impossible to determine who is ultimately responsible. While building this commune is dangerous work, Prado nevertheless feels that the resistance they have confronted means they are doing things right: communes that don't call into question the economic and political status quo, that don't make ambitious claims to land, and that don't put forward a radically new vision for Venezuelan society are simply not seen as a threat and can be ignored.

Despite clashing directly with elements of the state, however, communes like El Maizal cannot afford to reject the state as a whole, and their alliance with the national government remains essential. While El Maizal enjoys a degree of political strength and economic self-sufficiency, for Prado and others, the imperative for the movement is to grow or die. "We urgently need allies everywhere and to promote more communes because if El Maizal stands alone, *hermano*, or if this experience isn't born elsewhere, if it doesn't reproduce, the tendency will be toward failure, because there are just too many attacks."

The tense relationship with the state that characterizes El Maizal's history is echoed by many other communes. Much like El Maizal, organizers in the Ataroa Commune, in the blistering valley heat of urban Barquisimeto, didn't know that Chávez considered them a "priority" until he announced it one day on television. Even then, despite the attention it has brought, this priority status has not meant much in the way of concrete support. This may be for the better, as Ataroa today retains the fierce independence and bottom-up ethos of sustainability that marked its origins, if not its namesake. An indigenous leader, Ataroa—which means "he who watches from on high"—was said to have unleashed ferocious resistance against the Spanish in the mid-1500s, and those drawing inspiration from his name continue to fight today.

Ataroa Commune is a totally self-managed cluster of hexagonal buildings of different sizes around which well-worn footpaths wind and intersect. The space was originally a government sponsored "citizen participation center," but the name meant very little until the *comuneros* brought it to life. In 2006, well before the communes existed as a legal entity, radical organizers seized this space against the wishes of local Chavista leadership in order to make that participatory promise a reality by transforming it into a self-managed community center. Since then, they have repeatedly fought off co-optation and outright aggression, most recently from governor Henri Falcón, who was elected as a Chavista but has since joined the ranks of the opposition. According to one of Ataroa's spokespeople, Leonardo Ramos: "We fought for everything we have. That's why Falcón wouldn't dare to take it back— we would have a thousand people here in an hour." This history of ferocious autonomy serves as an antidote to government co-optation today: Ramos insists that "we never let the government tell us anything."

When the communal parliament gathers to make decisions under the welcome shade of the large central hexagon, this independence is on full display, beginning with the size of the crowd itself. A commune is technically governed by a parliament of delegates from each communal council and productive unit—a dozen or so, depending on the size of the commune. The hundreds gathered for debate at Ataroa were a testament to the fact that they are doing something different, that these *comuneros* are stretching and radicalizing the communal form in practice. Ramos is blunt: "We don't believe in the idea of a parliament," which relies on a representative structure. Instead, their parliamentary assembly is open, so that all members of every communal council are free to attend and participate in debate and discussion about the affairs of the community before the delegates vote.

Today, Ataroa is expanding its productive capacity. The commune directly manages a socialist enterprise that produces concrete blocks with high-quality machines bought with a low-interest government loan. Raw supplies aren't always easy to come by: cement was nationalized in 2008, which makes it affordable when it comes, but it is sometimes unavailable for months at a time. Sand is readily available on the private market but is very expensive. Still, Ramos boasts that the blocks are the cheapest and best available, and the workers, who propose both their own salaries and the cement block sale prices to the commune for collective approval, work only six-hour days.

The commune is currently developing more socialist enterprises to produce food and manage transportation for the local population. The space hosts a community information center that trains local youth in technological literacy on open-source computers and offers classes in both popular regional art and martial arts. In the center of the commune, a massive antenna juts out of the ground. While apparently out of place, it speaks to the strategic leverage the communes are wielding against the private sector. The antenna belongs to the private cellphone carrier Movistar, Ramos explains, but after taking over the space, the commune forced the corporation to pay rent, which covers the entire operating costs of its own radio station, Radio Crepuscular (Twilight Radio).

Today, the Ataroa Commune is looking expansively toward a communal future that displaces the private sector entirely rather than making deals with it. Next door, there is a huge, privately run market that sells food and other basic goods, but Ramos explains "it's a disaster" that doesn't serve the public good. Commune organizers are currently crafting an ambitious strategy that would use a potent aspect of the existing commune law as leverage to demand that the market be "transferred" to direct communal control. While this is far from guaranteed and approval depends on convincing a range of local and regional leaders, commune members are optimistic that they can make a compelling case that the transfer will serve the collective good.

As Ataroa and other nearby communes in Lara State seek ambitiously to expand the scope of their authority, they view communal media as a crucial ingredient for consolidating communal identity from below. Especially after the brief 2002 coup against Chávez, a network of popular media collectives flourished nationwide, working in parallel to the communal councils and communes and often oriented toward the same directly democratic goals. Ataroa in particular has been an epicenter of media struggles. Ataroa is also home to Lara TV, an important community television station that has existed for more than a decade. According to organizer Katrina Kozarek, for years this was a "community" station in name only, operating more like a family business. Tensions with the Ataroa Commune came to a head quickly, with the communal parliament deciding mid-session to seize the station immediately, for which they were scolded by the communications arm of the national government.

Commune organizers have since successfully pushed for elections to the leadership of Lara TV, previously limited to station workers, to include all members of the local communal councils. Ataroa and other communes have played a major role in nationwide debates on how to adjust media and communications to better fit a communal reality rather than simply reproducing capitalist culture. Today, these militant communicators are making demands similar to those that the communes make in the realm of economic production: that the media be neither private nor state-run but directly communal. More than simply reflecting the commune, popular grassroots media have a central role to play in stitching together an image of the communes for everyday Venezuelans and presenting them as a viable alternative.

All across the agricultural and industrial heartland of Venezuela, commune organizers are thinking beyond the law and beyond their local territories. Against the resistance of state governors—Chavista and opposition alike—and the private sector, the communes are beginning to craft regional unity from below in what are known as "political-territorial corridors" or "communal axes." Several such axes stretch across Lara and Venezuela as a whole. The Obelisco-Chirgua urban territorial corridor, for example, unites thirteen urban communes stretching across Barquisimeto.

Many others, such as the Fabricio Ojeda Corridor that stretches west from Lara into Portuguesa, take their names from Venezuela's long revolutionary history. One of the most important figures in overthrowing the Venezuelan dictatorship in 1958, Ojeda was later murdered in prison after joining the guerrilla struggle. Today, the Ojeda Corridor brings together eleven communes that produce an astounding 42 million pounds of coffee annually and nearly the same weight in bananas, 40 percent of which is produced by the 442 families of the Santa Clara Commune. To the east, four communes centering on Buría form a corridor named for the leader of the first successful slave revolution in Venezuela, Negro Miguel. And extending from the Ataroa Commune southward along the lush valley floor leading to Acarigua is the Argimiro Gabaldón Corridor, named for the epic guerrilla *comandante* who once roamed the nearby mountains, and which encompasses national park areas and strategic water sources before arriving at El Maizal.

In these territorial corridors and axes, we can begin to glimpse the emergence of a new communal state from below, just as the presidential council has begun to consolidate relations between the communes and the Bolivarian government from above. If communes bring together communal councils and communal cities bring together communes in a concentrated space, these communal corridors aspire toward the broader territorial integration of the communes. Coffee-producing communes exchange their product directly with those producing sugar, plantains, or beans, carving out an expanding space beyond the capitalist market. The goal, according to Alex Alayo, a member of the El Maizal Commune, is to establish a "new productive matrix" that would be able to move beyond basic goods and absorb industrial production.

Regional consolidation, Alayo argues, would bring with it the kind of economies of scale—the ability to produce more for less—on which capitalism itself thrives. Communes would share not only goods but technological advances, through popular education campaigns on the regional level. All of these gains would be maintained by popular self-defense networks like those of the collectives in the urban barrios. This expanded integration does not stop with the corridors, either: last year, several corridors in the region came together to formalize their political, social, and economic integration across three states. For Alayo, the urgent task of the present is to seize ever more space from below and to "communalize or even communize" these spaces through the creation of what he calls "free socialist territories" governed autonomously from below.

6

CULTURE AND PRODUCTION

El Cementerio has been a war zone for a long time. Stretching southwest from Caracas's Central University, this expansive jumble of barrios ends abruptly at, and is named for, the Cemetery of the South. It was here, in an area ominously called the New Plague, that the bodies of those slaughtered during the 1989 Caracazo were once dumped in a mass unmarked grave. Today this zone suffers a still newer plague, one shared by many barrios across Caracas and Venezuela as a whole: an epidemic of violence, often driven by territorial disputes over the drug trade.

Until recently, the Sin Techos barrio was one of the front lines of this war. The name Sin Techos refers to the homeless (literally "roofless") residents who once settled here. Only seven years ago, a street war with gangs in the nearby May First neighborhood claimed forty-seven lives, and when a group of young neighbors began to build a commune on this most inhospitable terrain, violence was the most pressing task to be resolved. Through slow and difficult work organizing and politicizing their neighbors, building relationships, and hosting cultural events, these twentysomethings were able to squash the beef with their neighbors, establishing a gang truce and bringing a level of peace to the barrio.

The experience of the Sin Techos Commune gets right to the heart of the challenges facing Venezuela's communes as a whole and urban communes in particular. Unlike the El Maizal and Ataroa communes, organizers in this dangerous corner of Caracas are much younger, are mostly men, and don't produce anything. This would seem like a contradiction: if the expanding network of communes is above all an attempt to build self-sufficient and self-governed communities, this task would seem impossible in those areas—especially in the cities—where no food has been grown and no goods have been produced in decades. The contradiction is even more complicated since the Bolivarian Revolution itself emerged out of the apparently unproductive terrain of the barrios. With more than 90 percent of Venezuelans living in cities, the challenge could seem insurmountable. How does a revolution work if people don't produce?

The question turns around many traditional Marxist dogmas about the revolutionary working class, but its importance is increasingly global in what Mike Davis has deemed our "planet of slums."[1] However, for Reinaldo Iturriza, who has been both commune minister and culture minister, to ask the question in this way is to get things backward, or at least to miss something crucial. For Iturriza, the commune is not only something that produces, but something that *is itself*

---

1   Mike Davis, *Planet of Slums* (London: Verso, 2006).

produced. Speaking at the ninth anniversary of the communal youth center Tiuna el Fuerte, in southern Caracas, he asked:

> What does it mean to produce the commune? There are people who say that the commune is something that produces potatoes, or *cachama* fish, or corn, as if the urban commune were an impossibility, as if the commune in Caracas or elsewhere were not a space where society is being produced, where culture is being produced, and where ideas are being produced too.

Culture, Iturriza insisted, "is not something that someone goes and buys in the supermarket, or something abstract that you find in books"; it is something "recreated permanently in the everyday."

Iturriza is not simply looking for a productive silver lining on otherwise unproductive terrain. In fact, the anniversary celebration at Tiuna el Fuerte was devoted to strategizing how to shift away from "rentism"—the cultural and economic dependence on oil—toward more self-sufficient forms of production. Instead, he points toward the creation of communal culture—an understanding and experience of living together, making democratic decisions together, and producing together—as a permanent task of all communes that no amount of corn or coffee production could replace. Chávez highlighted this very thing in his "Golpe de Timón" speech when he lamented the absence of the "*spirit* of the commune, which is much more important at this moment than the commune itself: communal *culture*."

After all, the young *comuneros* of barrio Sin Techos did not choose where to live or what battles to fight. They are organizing in the barrio because it is theirs, and they confronted the question of street violence because it was their problem most in need of immediate solutions. We should be clear, however, that they did produce something material, tangible, and concrete in the process: peace, safer streets, and an increased sense of community. Despite requesting resources from the state for specific projects, one commune activist, Manuel "Tití Bajo" Lugo, explains that the *comuneros* are above all "self-managed protagonists" who work autonomously on the local level. This new communal culture was not delivered to them by the state from above but built through their own slow work from below.

If anything, things have moved in the opposite direction, and their neighborhood organizing has served to inspire national policy. Building on their successful political work on the local level, the Sin Techos Commune spearheaded a program called Jovenes del Barrio (Barrio Youth). Hosting concerts, pick-up sports tournaments, and workshops to help local youth participate in small socialist enterprises, the Barrio Youth program has since gone national and become an integral part of the communal project, especially in urban areas. Since nine out of ten Venezuelans live in urban areas, there can be no network of communes without the cities, and there can be no communes in the cities without confronting the dangers that the urban poor face every day.

For Lugo, not only do the communes therefore need the barrio youth, but the reverse is also true: the communes, by creating spaces for local autonomy and self-governance, are the best chance many barrio youth have to confront the new plague of violence. Recent years have seen an increase in the drug trade, as narcotraffickers have made inroads into and even taken over entire barrios. Trapped between drug gangs and the police—the two often complicit and equally deadly—political organizing and new forms of production can offer an alternative for some. Translating national politics into barrio slang, Lugo argues that "building the commune is the *chamba*," the game, the hustle, both a stroke of luck and a pressing task.

Longtime militant Andrés Antillano leads a participatory research project in several communes of Caracas. Whereas many rural communes "function better because they are managing an existing productive function," he explains, "urban communes often come from sectors more excluded from production." Most residents work in the informal sector, buying and selling imported goods or working low-wage, part-time jobs, while those with jobs in the productive economy commute longer distances. Simply developing a communal culture does not resolve the question of production, however, and even where a commune does produce, political imbalances can result, as with the José Félix Ribas Commune high in the barrio of Antímano. There, a successful textile factory has had the effect of informally privileging the communal council that houses it and the individuals most directly involved in it, leading some other councils to break away from the commune in frustration.

For national commune coordinator Gerardo Rojas, who travels the country facilitating the establishment of new communes and troubleshooting the difficulties they confront in the process, "the urban commune is our biggest challenge in the present," in part due to cultural challenges specific to the cities and the barrios. Urban areas, he argues, breed individualism, separating and isolating people from one another and encouraging consumerism at the expense of the collective good. While the communes seek to establish a new form of directly democratic self-governance, Rojas worries that urban areas are antidemocratic in their very essence: "Cities aren't made for this, they are the invention of others." Moreover, to be in the cities—and in Caracas in particular— is to be closer to the state and its oil money, which encourages everyone to try to get their piece of the pie.

Some of the dangers this brings are obvious: rampant corruption and the tendency of political leaders to simply buy political loyalties with handouts rather than encouraging the community to participate. Many have pointed out the twin dangers whereby the government either resists grassroots organizing or co-opts it. Other challenges have emerged that are less obvious. For example, even where political officials have sought to support grassroots communal organizing from below, the mere presence of state funds has had unforeseen effects. Movements can become dependent on state funds in ways that affect their organizing, spending their energy engaging the government bureaucracy—applying for loans and filling out mountains of paperwork—instead of mobilizing the grassroots.

Moreover, especially where communes do not produce and thus have no resources of their own, there is a worrying trend toward competition between grassroots movements for state resources. This danger has crept up in El Cementerio. Ironically, not long after the young Sin Techos *comuneros* brokered the gang truce that brought relative peace to their neighborhood, they clashed with a nearby revolutionary collective. Since groups appeal to the government for funding based on their own organizational strength in local areas, the stakes of territorial control are high; in mid-2014, two members of the commune were killed.

While some on the left tend to assume that the state either supports movements, co-opts them, or represses them, the experience of the Venezuelan communes has been far more complex. State funding "immediately energizes and vitalizes popular organization," Antillano explains, but if seeking funding becomes a substitute for grassroots organizing, "it very quickly undermines that very organization it helped to facilitate," even without meaning to do so. Antillano evokes Greek myth to describe the curse of oil money as a never-ending "Sisyphean punishment": movements face an uphill struggle to access state resources only to find their organizing efforts rolling back downhill.

But despite this danger, Antillano is not among those purists who think that movements can afford to refuse state resources. That would simply be a political non-starter, in part because if they don't take the funds, someone else will. The real question is how to deal with the challenges of co-optation by and dependency on the state, and how best to use the funds to deepen self-management. There is no easy answer, Antillano insists: "You can do politics against the state or with the state, but you would be fucked trying to do politics without the state."

Other communes, like Pío Tamayo—located not far from Ataroa and El Maizal—have gone beyond merely embracing the cultural task of producing communal life. Despite being surrounded by factories and warehouses in the heavily industrial zone on the north side of Barquisimeto, these *comuneros* don't produce anything. At least not yet. Instead, they have sought to turn what appears to be a weakness into a strength by insisting that the best way to produce is to develop a solid revolutionary foundation first.

Named for an early precursor of Venezuelan communism, Pío Tamayo Commune brings together fifteen communal councils from the historically militant neighborhood of La Antena, a hotbed of the 1960s armed struggle. Many in this area were caught off guard by Chávez, although they quickly saw him for what he was: a reflection of the popular outrage against neoliberalism that exploded in the streets during the Caracazo. "He was like the child of the events of the 27th and 28th of February 1989," the *comunera* Nancy Perozo explained to me, so local residents took to the streets to support the failed coup of February 4, 1992, "and we the people still haven't returned to our homes."

The Pío Tamayo Commune came together around politics more than economics. Despite recognizing the need to produce, these *comuneros* are quick to point to the dangers of building communes around production, and of entering the economic realm without first developing political unity. Many communes, they argue, form around a communal business from the very beginning, leading some to divide or collapse from infighting over who will control either the communal businesses or the low-interest state loans they often bring. Without an accurate political compass, these old communists insist, corruption could lurk around any corner.

Moreover, the challenges faced by new productive enterprises are sometimes daunting. Often the government spearheads the efforts, identifying production priorities and providing start-up loans. If participants lack experience or cannot mobilize enough local participation, though, many of these projects quickly fold. Equally often, the problem is the market itself. Venezuela's reliance on oil means that the economy is flooded by cheap imported goods, which are steep competition for low-cost enterprises, especially if the goal is to pay workers a living wage.

Meanwhile, production is only a means, not the end. The goal is self-government—and to eventually replace the state with an alternative political structure, of which the communes are building blocks. New practices, ideas, and conceptions of power are crucial ingredients for this parallel, participatory state, and those can only be produced *"al calor del pueblo,"* in the heat of the people, in the words of commune spokesperson José Miguel Gómez. "We only accept accompaniment from the state, not leadership," says Gómez. "You don't consult with us, you debate politics with us." While some initially dismissed their approach as mere talk, developing political unity from the beginning has made Pío Tamayo more confident that their future economic projects will succeed. According to Gómez, "We are establishing communal politics to know how to manage the communal economy in a way that will bear fruit."

These militants may soon have a chance to test their theory in practice: when the Brazilian-owned Brahma Beer Corporation attempted to shutter a nearby factory in early 2013, more than 300 Brahma workers resisted the shutdown and occupied the factory, renaming it "Proletarians Unite." When workers brought the factory back into production, however, and began bottling water for local distribution, they were attacked by police, and opposition governor Henri Falcón cut their water off. The Pío Tamayo Commune, like Ataroa, is currently using the Commune Law—alongside direct political mobilizations—to pressure the government to transfer the factory to the direct control of the commune. The process has not been easy: court rulings have threatened to return the factory to private hands, and in March 2016 part of the factory was firebombed by unidentified assailants.

Urban communes have tackled the challenge of production in different ways. If Pío Tamayo has used their solid political foundation to ambitiously lay claim to a local worker-occupied factory, other urban communes have adapted to their socioeconomic terrain. Since the barrios are primarily spaces where goods and people circulate rather than sites of production, some communes have established transport and distribution collectives. Others have traced the contours of existing distribution networks by establishing socialist businesses to deliver goods from communes in the countryside to those in the cities. Still others have sought to jumpstart production by establishing socialist factories where nothing was produced before. The El Panal 2021 Commune has sought to do all of these at once.

This commune is located in the historically revolutionary 23 de Enero neighborhood of western Caracas, home to some of Venezuela's most radical movements. The area was originally under the control of the Alexis Vive Collective, one of the many collectives that took up arms to safeguard their neighborhood from drug violence and the police. Long before the communes existed, the collective envisioned armed self-defense as just one side of a broader process, so it was only natural that organizers would embrace the communal project as their own. Even today, the collective plays a central role in the commune from its headquarters, which boasts a large, three-dimensional model of the entire barrio and a wall of surveillance screens that oversee the security of the entire area. Spanning seven multicolored fifteen-story apartment blocks, along with the informal barrios that have sprung up between them, the commune incorporates 1,600 families and 12,000 local residents.

The name El Panal means "the honeycomb." Throughout the centuries, philosophers and economists have turned to bees as a metaphor to explain the potential and limitations of collective human activity. While some have done so to draw out the differences between bees and humans—arguing that bees naturally work together while people are naturally competitive—organizers here are more attuned to what they perceive as the similarities. For Robert Longa, the most visible representative of the Alexis Vive Collective and the El Panal Commune, the communal nature of bees proves that people too can live and produce together in equality and that there is no inherent contradiction between the individual and collective. Without an overarching plan or a strict hierarchical structure, a community of bees or humans alike can build a hive composed entirely of "perfect hexagons."

The honeycomb is the commune itself—the space constructed for directly democratic communal life—and the honey that fills it comes from the oil-funded social programs of the Venezuelan state: health care, education, sports, and cultural activities all enrich and nourish the local community. However, this harmonious image is not the whole story—after all, many organizers in El Panal are revolutionary communists who cut their teeth in armed self-defense. The community also has enemies, particularly the *zángano*, the unproductive, parasitic drones. While *zángano* can often refer to lazy people in general, members of El Panal understand the term to refer more specifically to the unproductive political and economic elites who have historically lived off the collective labor of the community. It is only by expelling the drones, Longa explains to me, that communal life can be rebuilt in a direct and participatory way as self-government among equals.

The name is fitting: El Panal is buzzing with productive activity, further proof that economic production is more effective when built on a solid foundation of political unity. Like Ataroa and other communes, El Panal began with popular media. The radio station, Arsenal Radio 98.1, has been transmitting music, political discussion, and news to the surrounding communities for more than a decade, and the commune's television studio is nearing completion as well. The commune, local organizer Sergio Gil explains, is "one big school," and this communication infrastructure plays a key role in an expanding educational curriculum that also includes youth art and music programs. A large new sports court is under construction, and these *comuneros* pride themselves on only hiring locally trained youth from the neighborhood: as Gil tells me, "The people do the work."

Organizers aim to incorporate the residents of all the towering apartment blocks as active participants in the everyday life of the commune and to further expand their productive base. The communal parliament currently manages a local bakery, a sugar-packaging plant, and a government-subsidized Mercal supermarket. A restaurant was recently opened, oriented not toward generating profit but toward building a sense of community by providing a self-sufficient service, low-cost student meals, and a space for local residents to congregate.

While consolidating production in its own territory, El Panal has also been extending feelers and deploying scout bees further afield to establish what members call *panalitos*, or "little honeycombs." While serving as mini-communes, these little honeycombs—mostly located in the countryside—are also nodes in a distribution network for basic goods like milk, beans, sugar, and corn flour, connecting the urban with the rural in direct exchange. A partnership with the Jirajara *campesino* movement in central-western Yaracuy State, for example, supplies the sugar-packaging plant in Caracas with the raw materials for a product often hard to find on supermarket shelves.[2] Recently, one of these little honeycombs—in Valencia, in Carabobo State—graduated to become a fully-fledged satellite commune with twelve communal councils of its own. As with other communes, all surplus is reinvested in the expansion and consolidation of the commune, allowing it to continue to expand as a self-sufficient unit. "We don't get anything from the government," one member explains.

Producing communal culture is about much more than political consciousness and collective coexistence, however. It cuts deeply into the complexities of Venezuela's colonial culture, which has always privileged white immigration and urban consumerism. As Venezuela became more "modern"—in other words, as it began to reflect the culture of Euro-American capitalism—many abandoned the countryside, and progress was increasingly measured in one's ability to consume imported goods: Italian pasta, Scotch whisky (Venezuela consumes more than any other Latin American country), and, more and more, electronics.

It was no coincidence that those who fought against colonial rule and slavery from the very beginning often did so by building communal societies beyond Spanish control, from traditional indigenous communities to the *cumbe* communities

---

2   Christina Schiavoni, "Competing Sovereignties in the Political Construction of Food Sovereignty," International Institute of Social Studies, January 24, 2014.

founded by runaway slaves. It is likewise no coincidence that those who today draw upon their inspiration continue to pioneer new forms of communal living and collective production that are compatible with older traditions, showing the ways that this new communal culture—by emphasizing local sustainability over consumerism—is also deeply anticolonial.

In the tiny Zancudo Commune deep in the southern Venezuelan flatlands, residents are experimenting with self-sufficient production and, in the process, with direct democracy. With the help of Walter Lanz, a nomadic organizer and founder of what he calls the Popular Fish-Farming School, the Zancudo Commune has spent the past few years learning how to raise a hearty fish called *cachama* in the water-filled ditches left behind by road construction. Like the ditches themselves, it is leftovers that feed the fish—scraps of yucca, squash, and plantain. The commune members invested zero, Lanz points out, and now they have a few thousand dollars—not an insignificant amount for this tiny community—to reinvest in their community. The surplus they have produced in the process has been more than economic, however—the fish have served as an organizing tool to bring the commune together and to generate a new and participatory collective identity. When they officially formed a commune, some of the teenagers whose only political education had been the process of cultivating the fish were elected as its spokespeople.

Lanz understands a central part of his job to be demystifying the process of raising the fish, proving in practice that no laboratory or technical expertise is required—a misconception that even the Chavista government has encouraged. "Even a child can raise *cachama*," he insists, giving an example of local problem-solving in action. When the water needed to be oxygenated for the fish to thrive, the community opted for a simple solution: they let the kids swim in it. The Chavista government is too focused on the macro level, Lanz maintains, emphasizing huge strategic industries and the mass production of specific consumer goods, "but we need small projects to fill the unproductive spaces."

Longtime militant intellectual José Roberto Duque spent years documenting and participating in popular struggles in Caracas before abandoning the bustle of the capital for rural life. Duque believes that "the commune should start with a single question: How are you going to finance it?" The question is not how to request government funding—as he puts it, "Government money is very weak cement for binding the community together"—but how to produce in a self-sustaining way that avoids reliance on the state. Duque argues that recent years have seen a profound cultural transformation that takes the commune back toward its precolonial origins and indigenous prototypes.

If the prevailing ideology since the 1950s has portrayed the cities as oases of modernity, it has simultaneously taught contempt for the countryside as a space for backward hillbillies. Old lifestyles became dirty words, icons of rural Venezuela to be laughed at and embarrassed by, and *conuco* was one such word. Not communes, strictly speaking, *conucos* are small, self-sustaining traditional farms where families produce the variety of crops they need to survive: a plantain tree here, some yucca, corn, and beans over there, all centering on a small, mud-walled shack. Once scorned, however, recent years have seen a new fondness and curiosity toward the countryside, and this had everything to do with Chávez.

Born in the country and steeped in its culture, Chávez was known to unexpectedly belt out country ballads on live television, helping to destroy the shame of the countryside and making people want to be farmers again. After all, contempt for the countryside was also a class disdain to be overcome alongside disdain for the residents of the urban barrios, many of whom originally came from the countryside. The role of the media in this transformation has been crucial, with media-content laws requiring that a certain percentage of broadcasting be nationally produced. This has led to a genuine rebirth of traditional musical forms. Whereas, in the past, national television might have featured mostly salsa, merengue, reggaetón, pop, and rock, today you might see music videos of flatland cowboys dancing a bouncy *joropo* accompanied by a harp and four-stringed *cuatro*, holiday *gaitas* from western Zulia State, and the Afro-Venezuelan *tambór* drumming especially predominant in coastal areas.

Once a dirty word, *conuco* is now being reclaimed. At the Ataroa Commune, for example, a new socialist business to raise natural pork at affordable prices has been named El Konuco. This term is just one of many. Escaped slaves once seized territories and built an early form of commune known as the *cumbe* to govern themselves autonomously and to launch attacks on the Spanish. Today the *cumbe* is being reborn, particularly in the historically Afro-Venezuelan coastal zone of

Barlovento east of Caracas, where autonomous slave communities held sway until the late eighteenth century. Commune
organizers in Barlovento are stretching the meaning of the
commune in practice by drawing upon these pre-existing
sources for inspiration to deepen the anticolonial tradition of
the commune. As a result, these Afro-*comuneros* have built
upon existing networks for communal chocolate production,
insisted on environmental sustainability, and even adopted a
local currency named for runaway slaves: *el cimarrón*.

Alongside Afro and indigenous communes, revolutionary
women also gathered recently in what is known as the National
School of Popular Feminism to brainstorm the establishment
of what they call antipatriarchal communes. Bringing together
representatives of twenty-five communes alongside international social movements, these organizers have supplemented
the basic communal vision of local self-government and
sustainable production with the insistence that a truly communal space would also challenge gender hierarchies, especially
with regard to care work. Communes, they argue, should
therefore include communal childcare and play areas and
grant women participatory control over contraception and
childbirth. Like many Afro and indigenous communes, moreover, these anti-patriarchal communes also tend to explicitly
embrace an ecological vision of sustainable relations to the
local environment.[3]

~

3   Cultura Nuestra, "The Meeting of a Feminist and Communal
School," *Venezuela Analysis*, October 19, 2015, venezuelanalysis.com.

More than five decades ago, hundreds of romantic young students abandoned the city for guerrilla warfare in the Venezuelan countryside, inspired by the Cuban Revolution and expecting that their own triumph would be just as quick. Today, many are repeating this pilgrimage to the country-side, but under no illusions that victory will be quick or easy—in part because they are fighting not a government but an entire culture. Nearly a decade ago, revolutionaries and rappers from the barrios of Caracas started to build their own communal homes and a self-sustaining village in rural Carabobo State known as Los Cayapos, whose name derives from an indigenous term for collective work. According to a young *comunera*, Mónica, who has participated in these back-to-the land movements: "We want to return to the country like our ancestors and do everything collectively like they did . . . This is not an isolated thing—thousands of us are thinking the same thing."

The ex-farmers who today constitute the majority of Venezuela's urban poor were forced off their land scarcely a half century ago. In the words of José Roberto Duque, "They seized us violently to create cities, the bourgeois state kidnapped us to make us cosmopolitan citizens less than a century ago, and it was bound to fail, because the prosperity of the cities was a myth and an illusion." Even today, he insists, many still "remember that they once had a country, and it wasn't full of shitty malls." The distance between the barrio residents and their recent ancestors, between revolutionary collectives on motorcycles and their rebellious indigenous and slave ancestors who once roamed the plains terrorizing elites on horseback, may not be so great after all.

Duque's vision is certainly as romantic as it is materialist. He himself has retreated to a small, out-of-the-way mountain town, above which he is slowly building a small home not of mud but of recycled garbage. He often carries plantains down to the town to exchange informally with friends and neighbors, living for weeks at a time on barter alone. Today, he explains, "there's a pressure toward the countryside, to grow something, to build a house. You don't need to put a gun to the heads of these young people like Pol Pot for them to go to the countryside. *This* is how the communal state will emerge."

CONCLUSION:
A COMMUNAL FUTURE?

In 2007, when Chávez was beginning to think seriously about uniting the already flourishing communal councils into communes, he turned to one of the "three roots" of what he had deemed the "tree" of Bolivarian ideology: the eclectic nineteenth-century utopian socialist and radical educator Simón Rodríguez. One of Bolívar's most important teachers and inspirations, Rodríguez spent much of his life in forced exile, where he took on the pseudonym "Robinson" after the title character of *Robinson Crusoe*.[1] According to the story, Crusoe was marooned off the Orinoco River delta—that is, just off the Venezuelan coast— eventually enslaving a native Carib whom he named Friday. Rodríguez too was stranded far from home and, like many others, he found in the character of Crusoe an example of popular, practical self-education.

---

1   Richard Gott, *Hugo Chávez and the Bolivarian Revolution* (London: Verso, 2011), 102–9.

Long after the death of his most famous pupil, Rodríguez laid out a characteristically ambitious vision for an ideal Latin American republic that has become a mandatory reference point today, evoking old debates about the transition to socialism while providing a specifically Venezuelan response. In an 1847 letter, Rodríguez urged the destruction of the existing religious and military powers dominating Venezuela and their replacement with a system of decentralized local rule that he called "toparchy." Fusing the theories of European socialism with the concrete reality of Latin America's indigenous communal history, Rodríguez wrote that each of these small, self-governing units would be united in a broad confederation that he deemed "the most perfect form of government for those who can imagine a better politics."

Today, the concept of toparchy has been resuscitated as an innovative contribution to longstanding debates around the viability of small "islands of socialism" amid a vast and turbulent capitalist sea, although in Venezuela, past and present, these islands would be less isolated and populated by far more Fridays than Crusoes. For former commune minister Reinaldo Iturriza, the communes represent "trenches from which we battle to build our very particular, incomparable, and 'toparchic' version of socialism. And you can be sure that there are more: places that we haven't yet arrived, experiences we haven't known."[2]

---

2   Reinaldo Iturriza, "Desear la comuna," *El Otro Saber y Poder*, August 22, 2013), elotrosaberypoder.wordpress.com.

To embrace toparchy is not, however, to romanticize dispersed, local power but to recognize—humbly and with eyes wide open—the starting point and to realistically map the terrain of struggle. It is also crucially to strategize the consolidation and unification of a more ambitious communal system. The description of the communes as a toparchic network of local self-government has gained a surprising degree of traction in the present. It is not only evoked in speeches by political leaders but also emerges organically from many commune organizers as the most apt description of both the process and the goal, the means and the end.

For example, at a communal space in Terrazas de Cúa, in a lush valley more than an hour south of Caracas, the local collective bears the name Toparcha, and the bony dog that scoots around this budding commune is affectionately called Topo. What was once a war zone has been replaced by an impressive communal space: a pristine, covered sports court alongside a large and well-equipped children's playground, all designed and installed communally by the neighbors themselves. The *comuneros* manage a community garden full of peppers, garlic, and herbs, and the younger participants recently built a recording studio out of superadobe, which today stands adorned with a mural of revolutionary folk singer Alí Primera.

Miranda State, where they are located, has been in opposition hands for the past eight years, and the governor is none other than opposition presidential candidate Henrique Capriles. However, as commune organizer Rosa Capote explains, some of the most powerful enemies of the commune wear red: it was the local Chavista mayor, fearing a loss of influence, who sought to prevent them from registering as a commune. As a result, their experience has, ironically, been the opposite of many other communes. They were a real commune for years but have only recently managed to register officially.

Despite clashing with powerful Chavistas in practice, these commune organizers are faithful to the revolutionary process as a whole and understand themselves to be the best guarantors of that process. They are the ones building sustainable local communities and encouraging grassroots participation; they are the ones doing the hard work of rebuilding Venezuela from the bottom up. If the Bolivarian Revolution falters—as it appears to be doing at present—the experience of building a commune without governmental support and on hostile terrain gives these grassroots militants confidence that they can continue to build. "The revolution no longer depends on the government," a teenaged *comunero* in Terrazas de Cúa proudly declares to me. If the Maduro government were to disappear tomorrow, "this will still be here regardless."

The revolutionary youth organization Otro Beta has played a major support role not only for this small communal island but for other parts of Miranda. And if the experience of building a commune against the odds has strengthened the revolutionary resolve of organizers in Terrazas de Cúa, trying to consolidate a broader communal structure across the inhospitable terrain of this opposition-governed state has made a toparchic approach mandatory. Miranda, Venezuela's most densely populated state, contains barrios like Petare and lush rural zones stretching toward Cúa, but also the wealthy urban and suburban areas that feed the opposition's local dominance. On this varied and resistant terrain, the communal project has taken a very different form. What has emerged instead is a network of small communal spaces and socialist enterprises that are connected only from a distance.

The Commune Law was designed above all to consolidate local power in specific areas, but this means it is not particularly well suited to building relationships at a distance. Otro Beta organizers therefore understand their role as helping to integrate a strategic exchange network among a number of dispersed islands of socialist participation and production. They travel constantly throughout the region, facilitating exchanges between communal councils and socialist enterprises, helping local organizers navigate the formalities of state bureaucracy, and raising consciousness about the communal project. By connecting a textile cooperative to a commune in need of school uniforms, for example, or by building a relationship between rural plantain farmers and communal councils in urban areas, they are beginning to knit together a sort of vast communal web. "We want to unify all of Miranda," organizer Jorge Vilalta explains.

Such a project would not be legally recognized as a commune, since the law stipulates that those involved in a commune must occupy the same space. It is nevertheless a key ingredient— arguably the key ingredient—to a broader communal reality in which participation is more important than formal legal requirements, and which urgently needs unity if it hopes to survive. Nancy Perozo, a spokesperson for the Pío Tamayo Commune, describes the communal project as "a network, like weaving a spider web, a fabric that moves from the communal councils to the communes to the territorial axes . . . We will advance toward the communal cities and then on to socialism throughout the entire homeland." This image of stitching together a vast communal fabric makes it clear that what is under way in Venezuela is about far more than mere decentralization or simply localized self-government.

According to commune coordinator Gerardo Rojas, decentralization—one of the keywords of neoliberal reform—is a "right-wing discourse," whereas the emerging communal state seeks to consolidate power from the opposite direction, "aggregating from below." If Venezuela's communes are territorial institutions aimed at gradually reclaiming space from capitalism, the challenges posed by territory are among the most serious. Like the nodes dispersed across Miranda, even established communes can find it difficult to unify local space as the law requires. For example, Ataroa Commune suffered a serious division after a political clash that led ten of the forty-two communal councils to the west to break away from the commune. Legally, these new councils could not constitute a new commune; it was only through sheer luck that Ataroa retained enough councils for the communal parliament to continue to function with a quorum.

However, territory is also the communes' most important strength. The tactical genius of the Occupy Movement, the

Spanish *indignados*, and those who gathered in Egypt's Tahrir Square was to seize space, democratize it, and refuse to leave. For many commune organizers across Venezuela, the task of the communes is similar: to seize space and territorialize socialism as the only possible guarantee for the future.

Can the communal state actually displace the existing state? When I spoke with vice minister of communes Rosángela Orozco in 2014, she hesitated before answering this question: "Should I answer for the ministry, or as a militant?" For Orozco, a veteran of the Alexis Vive Collective, the communes do not exist to simply do the bidding of the existing state: "The communes are made to govern, but what worries us is that we have a capitalist state that refuses to die." The Bolivarian Revolution already has too many external enemies to create internal ones, so despite Maduro's open insistence on the need to "demolish the bourgeois state," in practice the government has tended to skirt the question of the inherent conflict brewing between the traditional state and this new communal "state."

Roland Denis has no such hesitations: the communal state is, in his view, really just "a camouflaged name for the communist state." This answer only begs more questions, since Marx described the Paris Commune as "a revolution against the State itself."[3] "That's where we enter into all of the contradictions of the term—what state, if we are actually talking about a nonstate?" says Denis. "The communes could

---

3   Marx, *The Civil War in France*, first draft (April–May 1871).

create a productive capacity that begins to compete with capitalism, with its own internal rules and logic, and this could really progressively generate a nonstate."

This competition between the traditional state and the communes is already beginning to emerge. For Alex Alayo of the El Maizal Commune, the traditional state and the communal state currently coexist (uncomfortably) as two fundamentally different powers. On one hand, there is a popular government in a bourgeois state structure; on the other hand, this expanding network of free territories is "building a new state" from below. The tensions and "frictions" that arise in such a situation are inevitable, and will only increase if the communes continue to expand. "We are fighting an outright war against the traditional bourgeois state," Alayo adds. If popular struggles are co-opted and captured by the traditional state, even in subtle ways, the Venezuelan Revolution might share the fate of the Mexican Revolution more than a century ago, about which a general once joked that "this revolution has degenerated into a government." For Alayo, "the institutionalization of the revolution means the death of the revolution." In some senses, he even worries that "the revolution has stopped . . . Whether it will move forward or not depends on the people."

Recent months have seen sharp reminders of this tension between the new and the old, with the most conservative elements of the existing state launching counterattacks at the very heart of the communal "state" in development. Organizers continue to be harassed and arrested, and most worryingly, the appeals chamber of the Supreme Court even briefly revoked the agrarian charter for El Maizal Commune after the former owners claimed that the lands had not been idle and therefore should not have been expropriated. Social movements and President Maduro himself quickly attacked the legal maneuver, leading the Court's constitutional chamber to put the decision on hold, but the question remains as to whether or not, without Chávez, the communes will have the support they need to survive the inevitable assault from reactionary forces within and outside Chavismo.

The challenges the communal project faces are many: the economic challenge of production, especially in the urban barrios; the political challenges posed by the anti-Chavista opposition and from within Chavismo; and the cultural challenge of breaking with oil-fueled consumerism and moving toward a sustainable economy built upon a collective culture. Let no one suggest that building the Venezuelan commune is anything but a battle against all odds. Yet the fact that the battle is even possible means that much has changed since the Venezuelan poor explosively rejected neoliberalism in 1989.

Where some can only see impossibility, those organizing on the ground know that they have no choice but to fight to build this concrete alternative, using whatever leverage they have. They are finding this leverage in the most unexpected places. The words of Chávez and the laws his government approved have provided important new weapons for consolidating those communes that emerged before the law and that today transcend the law itself. Chávez's last major speech, the "Golpe de Timón," made perfectly clear that to be a Chavista is to be a *comunero*, and it has become a near-universal reference point to legitimize the communal project.

Beyond this, and beyond even the promise of popular participation enshrined in the Constitution, organizers are using the Commune Law ambitiously to demand the transfer of power from private and state hands directly to the communes themselves. While this often depends on the particular constellation of local leadership, many *comuneros* are using this provision to expand their authority and prove that they can govern themselves more efficiently than either the private or public sectors. Furthermore, every municipality nationwide is currently required to renovate its local public planning council to include direct representation from nearby communes. While these councils—which exercise oversight over the municipal budget—have often been stacked by local mayors, today they may be a key battleground in the conflict between the old state and the new.

Arguably the most important leverage for the communes comes from the crisis itself, however. The period since Chávez's death has seen the stable economic growth of previous years suddenly unravel, giving way to a spiraling currency crisis, inflation, and acute shortages of some basic goods. For this, the collapse in global oil prices is partly to blame, but more so the longstanding failure to break oil dependency by stimulating domestic production. This is a century-old contradiction, and the problem is in the system, not in the government, as the opposition would argue. However, in recent years, a rigid system of currency controls has encouraged an outright epidemic of black-market speculation, smuggling, and hoarding that has also played a part in the devastation.

Corruption at the intersection of the state and the private sector remains a plague that Chavismo has not been able to eliminate. In 2012 alone, some $20 billion simply disappeared into the black hole of the private import sector—money that was meant to fill the country's shelves but instead lined the pockets of corrupt speculators, and presumably some state officials as well. Recent estimates suggest that up to 40 percent of all food produced in or imported into Venezuela is smuggled across the border to be resold elsewhere for much higher prices, along with $4 billion worth of gasoline annually.[4] It is this massive fraud and corruption that the government denounces as an "economic war," although it is motivated by political reasons as often as economic ones.

It may seem contradictory to suggest that the communes might benefit from the crisis. After all, as oil resources rapidly dry up, they suffer. But as the crisis deepens and the corrupt import sector continues to prove untrustworthy, the communes may begin to look increasingly attractive as a stable, productive foundation for the Bolivarian Revolution. Because they produce what communities need locally, many *comuneros* see themselves as the best weapon against the economic war. "The state hasn't measured up," Ángel Prado of El Maizal argues, boasting that El Maizal is twenty times

---

4 "Contrabando hacia Colombia agudiza escasez en Venezuela," *Portafolio*, February 14, 2014, portafolio.co.

more productive with fewer resources than either the private sector or the state.[5] Recent months have seen new mechanisms that allow the communes to sidestep importers entirely by directly importing necessary raw materials, not to mention ambitious proposals for exerting participatory communal control over the import sector.[6] Imagine what the communes could do with $20 billion!

The question mark looming over the future of the Maduro government just might provide the best possible catalyst for the communes—and for the revolutionary grassroots as a whole. Despite the catastrophic electoral defeat of December 2015, which gave the right-wing opposition a two-thirds supermajority in the National Assembly (and with it the power to stack the Supreme Court, to use the Court to impeach the president, and to call a Constituent Assembly to rewrite the 1999 Constitution), the country remains heavily Chavista.[7] Many voters who turned against the government did so to punish leaders for failing to correct the economy—they did not buy into the "economic war" narrative, and if the government's strategy was to

---

5   There is good reason to believe that self-managed production can be just as productive as private or state production, if not more so. See Dario Azzellini, ed., *An Alternative Labour History: Worker Control and Workplace Democracy* (London: Zed, 2015).

6   For the best account of the causes of the Venezuelan economic crisis, as well as necessary currency reforms, see Mark Weisbrot, *Failed*, chapter 5. According to Weisbrot, the crisis provoked a sharp decrease in imports that could also favor domestic communal production in the long run.

7   As I write this, the opposition's two-thirds supermajority has been put on hold by the Supreme Court amid allegations of electoral fraud in several districts.

delay unpopular economic reforms in order to win elections, this strategy has been a colossal failure.

The defeat is a symptom of the bureaucratization of the Bolivarian process and the strained relation between the grassroots and the leadership. For now, the Chavistas stare down a hostile legislature that is intent on removing them from power once and for all. The opposition that regularly denounced Chávez as a dictator is making the most of the expanded democracy that Chavismo created, collecting the millions of signatures required to hold a recall referendum that, if held before the end of 2016, would trigger new elections if Maduro is defeated. The possibility of Maduro's ouster may provide the best incentive for the revolutionary grassroots to jumpstart and accelerate the building of autonomous spaces, seizing new territories from which to resist the return of the right. As I chat with some hardline comrades in Petare, one young woman who cut her teeth amid the drug trade and gang warfare rife in the barrios of Caracas is more willing than most to speak the unspeakable: "Maybe it would better if we lost the election. Then we'll know right away who's with us and who's against us."

It would be foolish to suggest that things have not changed dramatically since the death of that dynamic center of Venezuela's Bolivarian process, Hugo Chávez, or to deny the economic crisis of the present, the spiraling currency and spiking inflation, and the creeping corruption and military power it has wrought. Equally foolish, however, is the implication—shared by nearly all mainstream press coverage at the time of Chávez's death—that with him, so too died the Bolivarian process. This was never a one-man show; to suggest otherwise is an insult to those who were building the revolution decades before Chávez, and an insult to those who continue to build revolutionary power today.

Still capitalist, not yet socialist, Venezuela stands uncomfortably between two economic systems and two different states, with the contradictions of each reaching a fever pitch. The construction and consolidation of grassroots power from below in Venezuela has been a long and arduous process, stretching across decades. Today, this alternative power emerging from below, this dual power, is seeking out an alternative space in the communes in which to make the long-promised revolution a concrete reality. But this power does not ultimately escape the imperative Lenin once assigned to it: it must tip eventually to one side or the other. As time runs out, the tipping point rushes to greet us.

The time has come to bet it all on the communes. While this may seem risky, the alternative is to bet on nothing at all. The middle class, the *ni-nis* (neither-nors) in the center, the parasitic bourgeoisie, the state bureaucracy, a Socialist Party incapable of winning elections, and an increasingly corrupt military—who could possibly save the process but those who have saved it on every other occasion? "If the government—with all of the challenges of imports, hoarding, and prices—is fucked, who else can solve this?" asks Ángel Prado of El Maizal. "We can, the communes . . . because we don't depend on the state." As goes the commune, so goes the Bolivarian Revolution as a whole. As Chávez himself put it, and as every passing day confirms, the choice is increasingly between *la comuna o nada*, the commune or nothing.

ACKNOWLEDGEMENTS

Thanks above all to the members of the Popular Territories research group in Caracas: Andrés Antillano, Mila Ivanovic, Guillermo Pérez, Victor Pineda, Ivan Pojomovsky, Doris Ponce, Enrique Rey, and Chelina Sepúlveda. Thanks to Gerardo, Estela, Luis, Gabriela, Toti, and Duque for all their help and generous hospitality. I am grateful to those who took the time to read a manuscript that differed dramatically from this final version, thanks in no small part to their insightful comments: Federico Fuentes, Michael Lebowitz, Louis Philippe Römer, Naomi Schiller, and Alejandro Velasco. Consistent thanks for the support of those helping to slow the advance of the neo–Chicago Boys, for whom any crisis is an opportunity: in particular, Keane Bhatt, Greg Grandin, Miguel Tinker Salas, Greg Wilpert, Mark Weisbrot, and the unflagging staff of Venezuela Analysis and TeleSUR. Thanks to James Martel and Jodi Dean for supporting an early version of what became this book project, to Bhaskar Sunkara for his encouragement and guidance, and to Audrea Lim for helping shepherd it into reality. Thanks to *Jacobin* magazine and *Roar* magazine, where some of these words first appeared. This research was funded in part by the Antelo Devereux Award for Young Faculty provided by Drexel University's College of Arts and Sciences. Thanks, finally and most importantly, to all those *comuneras* and *comuneros*, in Venezuela and beyond, who continue to fill our horizon with new content, deciphering the sphinx as they build it.

Printed in the United States
by Baker & Taylor Publisher Services